Mighty Fine Motor Fun

by Christy Isbell

Dedication
This book is dedicated to my mother. I love you—Christy

Acknowledgments
Thank you to the Early Learning Program of East Tennessee State University's Child Study Center for your willingness to allow me to visit your classrooms and take photographs.

Special Thanks
Sheila P. Smith—Thank you for editing the book and for being the "queen of organization."
Michael O. Talley—Your photographs of the beautiful young children at play make the book come alive!
Ann Marie Cornelison, Joy Matson, Charity Clark, and Erin Rudd—Thank you for sharing your knowledge of teaching young children with me.

Mighty fine Motor fun

Fine Motor Activities for Young Children

Gryphon House
Silver Spring, MD

Christy Isbell
Illustrated by Chris Wold Dyrud
Photographs by Michael O. Talley

© 2010 Christy Isbell
Published by Gryphon House, Inc.
10770 Columbia Pike, Suite #201, Silver Spring, MD 20901
800.638.0928; 301.595.9500; 301.595.0051 (fax)

Visit us on the web at www.gryphonhouse.com

Illustrations: Chris Wold Dyrud
Photographs: Michael O. Talley

Library of Congress Cataloging-in-Publication Information
Isbell, Christy.
 Mighty fine motor fun / by Christy Isbell ; Illustrated by Chris Wold
Dyrud ; Photographs by Michael O. Talley.
     p. cm.
 Includes bibliographical references.
 ISBN 978-0-87659-079-9
 1. Motor ability in children. 2. Language arts (Preschool). 3. Writing.
 I. Dyrud, Chris Wold. II. Title.
 RJ133.I83 2010
 152.3--dc22

Bulk purchase
Gryphon House books are available for special premiums and sales promotions as well
as for fund-raising use. Special editions or book excerpts also can be created to
specification. For details, contact the Director of Marketing at Gryphon House.

Disclaimer
Gryphon House, Inc. and the author cannot be held responsible for damage, mishap, or
injury incurred during the use of or because of activities in this book. Appropriate and
reasonable caution and adult supervision of children involved in activities and
corresponding to the age and capability of each child involved is recommended at all
times. Do not leave children unattended at any time. Observe safety and caution at all
times.

Table of Contents

Chapter 1: What Are Fine Motor Skills and Why Are They Important? 7

Introduction 7

What Fine Motor Skills Should
   Preschoolers Have? 8

How Do Young Children Develop
   Their Fine Motor Skills? 9

   Developmental Sequence of Fine
     Motor Skills 10

   Cultural and Gender
     Considerations 11

   The Foundations of Fine Motor
     Skills 11

Development of Pre-Writing and
   Pre-Scissor Skills 14

   Sequence of Pre-Writing 14

   Sequence of Pre-Scissor Use 15

Chapter 2: Getting Started: The Importance of the Environment . . .17

   How to Guide Pre-Writing Skills . . .18

   Developmental Steps for
     Learning Pre-Writing 18

Hands at Play 19

Using Learning Centers to Encourage Fine
   Motor Development 20

   Fine Motor Center 21

   Layout of the Fine Motor Center . . .22

   Props for the Fine Motor Center . . .24

Just the "Write" Size: Selecting Tools and
   Materials .25

Chapter 3: Fine Motor Activities for Three-Year-Olds 29

What Can Most Three-Year-Old Children Do
   with Their Hands? 29

Activities
BILATERAL HAND SKILLS
Marble Painting 31

Moving Bubbles 32

Toy Workshop 33

Twinkle, Twinkle, Little Star 34

DRAWING
Floor Drawing 35

EYE-HAND COORDINATION
Styrofoam Construction 36

GRASP
Corn Picking 37

Squeezy Water Play 38

Stamp Art 39

Vertical Board Play 40

GRASP AND RELEASE
Mini-Muffin Sorting 41

HAND STRENGTH
Hide and Seek Play Dough 42

Sand Castle Clay 43

PRE-SCISSOR SKILLS
"Pop" Straws 44

Card Cutting 45

Clothespin Airplanes 46

Shredded Paper Collage 47

Squirt Game 48

Tong Pick-Up 49

PRE-WRITING SKILLS
Body Shapes 50

Cardboard Stencils 51

No-Mess Finger Painting 52

Racing Tracks 53

Wall Washing 54

Yarn Shapes 55

STRINGING/LACING
Cup Tower 56

Ribbon Pull .57

Shish-Kabob Snack 58

Straw Jewelry 59

UPPER BODY STRENGTH
Walk Like an Animal 60

Chapter 4: Fine Motor Activities for Four-Year-Olds 61

What Can Most Four-Year-Old Children Do
   with Their Hands? 61

Activities
COLORING
Crayon Rubbings 64

EYE-HAND COORDINATION
Dressing Up 65

Finger Puppets 66

Photo Puzzles 67

GRASP
Cookie Decorating 68
Drops of Color 69
Reusable Stickers 70
Seed Art 71
Stick Houses 72
Tape It Up! .73

HAND STRENGTH
All-Terrain Vehicles 74
More Peas Please 75

PRE-SCISSOR SKILLS
Disappearing Holes 76
Making a Wreath 77
Paper Chains 78
Place Mats .79

PRE-WRITING SKILLS
Feely Shapes 80
Glue Shapes and Letters 81
Incline Writing Boards 82
Journal Drawing 83
Mirror, Mirror, on the Wall 84
Ribbon Drawing 85
Shape Person 86
Sidewalk Shadows 87
Simon Says 88

STRINGING/LACING
Bead Jewelry 89
Make Your Own Lacing Cards 90
Tambourine 91

TOOL USE
Hair Salon and Barber Shop 92
Kite Flying .93
Making a Collage 94
Polka-Dot Shapes 95

Chapter 5: Fine Motor Activities for Five-Year-Olds 97
What Can Most Five-Year-Old Children
    Do with Their Hands? 97

Activities
BILATERAL HAND SKILLS
Geoboards .99

EYE-HAND COORDINATION
Graph Paper Art 100
Making Tracks 101

Stick Letters 102
Paper Flowers 103

FINGER ISOLATION
Where is Thumbkin? 104

GRASP
Clay Writing Board 105
Cotton Swab Painting 106
"Itsy Bitsy" Writing Utensils 107
Water Droppers 108

IN-HAND MANIPULATION
Coin Match 109
Piggy Banks 110

PRE-WRITING SKILLS
Furry Letters 111
Glitter Letters 112
Rainbow Letters 113
Sandbox Writing 114
Sandpaper Writing 115
Write a Little Note 116

PUZZLES
Make Your Own Puzzle 117

SCISSOR SKILLS
Animal Masks 118
Paper Dolls 119
Paper Mobile 121
Snowflakes 122

STRINGING/LACING
Lace Up Those Shoes 123

TOOL USE
Clay Sculptures: Self-Portrait 124
Magic Rocket 125
Nature Prints 126
Off to Work I Go! 127
Painted Flower Pots 128
Treasure Box 129

Chapter 6: Answers to Questions from Preschool Teachers 131
Glossary 135
References 137

Chapter 1

What Are Fine Motor Skills and Why Are They Important?

Introduction

Young children are naturally curious. They learn about the world by interacting with their peers and by exploring objects and materials with their hands. During their early years, children develop the hand skills (fine motor skills) they will need in order to be successful at play and work for the rest of their lives. In addition, young children learn to use their hands for important self-care skills, such as feeding and dressing themselves.

Preschoolers use fine motor skills throughout the day. At circle or group time, a preschooler may use her hands to clap along with the music, do fingerplays, or point at a picture. During learning center time, she may use her hands to put on dress-up clothes, wash a doll, turn the pages of a book, stack blocks, draw, cut with scissors, or pick up toys. At snack time, she may use her hands to eat dry cereal, pour milk, and drink from a cup. In short, a quality preschool classroom offers a young child many opportunities to explore and develop her fine motor skills.

Research-based teaching practice incorporates a wide range of strategies to help children develop fine motor skills in preschool classrooms. Many states have set standards for Pre-K programs, with guidelines that include fine motor development. Teachers use these state standards to guide their decisions about which activities, tools, and materials to introduce to young children before they enter kindergarten. State Pre-K standards typically suggest that a successful learning environment gives children opportunities to use age-appropriate tools as well as have the chance to write, draw, and experiment with a variety of art materials.

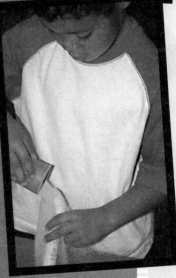

Preschoolers need daily experience with developmentally appropriate fine motor activities so they can build the confidence and skills they will need later in life (Bredekamp & Copple, 2009). In a high-quality preschool, teachers provide ample opportunities for children to participate in drawing, cutting, gluing, stringing, and manipulating objects with their hands. In elementary school, children further refine their fine motor skills as they participate in handwriting, computer keyboarding, science experiments, and more complex art projects.

What Fine Motor Skills Should Preschoolers Have?

By the time they arrive in preschool, most children should be able to perform the following basic fine motor actions (Exner, 2005):

* **Reach**: Moving her arm forward to grasp or touch an object.
* **Grasp**: Using her fingers to get an object into her hand.
* **Carry**: Using her hand to move an object from one place to another place.
* **Release**: Letting go of an object she holds in her hand.
* **In-Hand Manipulation**: Using her fingers to adjust an object inside her hand.
* **Bilateral Hand Use**: Using her two hands together in an activity.

Several factors influence the development of a child's fine motor skills. Young children need good vision to be able to see the materials they use in fine motor activities, as well as to understand the movements involved in the activities. The term **eye-hand coordination** describes this strong relationship between vision and fine motor skills. Preschoolers also use their **tactile** (touch) sense and their **proprioceptive** (body position) sense to help learn how to use their hands. A child's cognitive development affects her ability to manipulate objects and explore how to use new tools and materials. If a child has delayed or impaired cognitive, visual, or tactile awareness, that delay may have a significant effect on her ability to develop her fine motor skills.

Terms in bold are defined in the glossary, which begins on page 135

How Do Young Children Develop Their Fine Motor Skills?

Preschoolers develop fine motor skills through play with appropriate materials and objects. Preschoolers also learn through repetition and experimentation. A learning environment with a wide variety of open-ended materials such as paper, drawing utensils, glue, clay, and small blocks provides a young child with a variety of opportunities to explore her own interests. Preschoolers who have the chance to construct their own knowledge and who can work at their own levels will be more engaged in learning and more capable of developing their fine motor skills (Bredekamp & Copple, 2009).

When a young child participates in an activity that helps develop her fine motor skills, the product of that activity is not as important as the process. A preschooler must be free to express herself through her exploration of new materials. For instance, giving a four-year-old child a blank piece of paper, a choice of several different paintbrushes, and a set of watercolor paints will provide more interesting ways for the child to practice her fine motor skills than offering the child a coloring book and crayons. It is important to remember that each child creates differently. When a class of preschoolers finishes a fine motor activity, their products should not all look alike. Variety in finished products shows that teachers are encouraging the children to participate in fine motor activities as unique individuals; this describes **developmentally appropriate practice**.

Although preschoolers typically develop their fine motor skills while interacting with their peers, they also can learn crucial fine motor skills from adults. Adults can "teach" or demonstrate to a young child how to use a new tool, such as an eyedropper or a 1-hole punch. When you introduce a new tool to a child, keep your instructions simple and brief. Clearly demonstrate the basic ways to use the tool or material, then give the child time to explore how she can use the tool.

If there are safety precautions that relate to using a certain object or material, it is important that you include a brief discussion of the safety procedures before sharing the activity. Generally, one or two "safety tips" are all that a preschooler can remember. Try to keep the suggestions positive in nature. Simply explain how the child can use the tool or material safely. See Chapter 2 for more information on selecting appropriate tools and materials for preschoolers. Here are some examples of how to introduce appropriate safety tips for different materials:

● Glue
Today, we will use glue to stick _____ (tissue, cardboard, and so on) to _____ (paper, and so on).
● Stapler
We use a stapler to fasten papers together.
Watch your fingers! Keep them on top of the stapler.
● Scissors
We use scissors at the table.
Today, we are cutting _____ (paper, string, and so on) with scissors.

Developmental Sequence of Fine Motor Skills

Young children develop their fine motor skills in a general sequence. This sequence begins during the third month of life and progresses until the child develops mature fine motor patterns (typically during the later elementary-school years). Here is the basic sequence of fine motor development:

Large to Small: An infant can grasp large objects like a rattle (5 months) before she learns to grasp small objects like a small peg (12 months).

Palm to Finger: An infant begins by grasping objects in the palms of her hands. She then progresses to holding small objects with her fingertips. Most two-year-old children hold markers in the palms of their hands, whereas most five-year-old children can hold a pencil with their thumb and fingertips.

Hands Together to Hands Separately: At first, a child's two hands do the same thing at the same time. A nine-month-old baby can clap her hands together; by age three, she is starting to develop **reciprocal hand skills**, where one hand does one thing while the other hand does something different. For example, a four-year-old child can hold paper in one hand and cut a straight line through that paper with the other hand.

Because each child develops at her own pace, you will see differences in children's rates of development. Several factors may influence a child's fine motor development, such as muscle tone, body build, and temperament. However, the above sequence of fine motor development is typical for the majority of young children (Henderson & Pehoski, 2006; Thelen & Smith, 1994).

Cultural and Gender Considerations

Children across all cultures will ultimately develop similar fine motor abilities. However, culture can have an impact on the speed at which a young child acquires different motor skills. Some cultures place a greater emphasis on active play and gross (large) motor activities than on fine (small) motor activities such as drawing or cutting with scissors. Children of some cultures may not have access to toys or the opportunity to use materials such as writing and drawing tools that would facilitate fine motor development. As a result, it may take some preschoolers longer to develop their fine motor skills or specific tool use (Case-Smith, 2005;Trawick-Smith, 1997).

Other cultures place a high value on young children's fine motor development. For example, Chinese preschool programs routinely provide activities that encourage young children's use of scissors, writing utensils, and painting tools. Some Chinese three-year-olds have such advanced fine motor skills that they can cut intricate snowflakes out of thin paper and participate in very small origami projects.

Research suggests that gender differences also exist in the way children acquire fine motor skills. Girls are frequently more competent than boys of the same age at performing fine motor skills, such as drawing and cutting with scissors. Discrepancies between the genders exist in handwriting particularly. Girls are more likely to write faster and more legibly than boys of the same age (Trawick-Smith, 1997; Tseng & Cermack, 1993; Tseng & Chow, 2000).

The Foundations of Fine Motor Skills

Three- and four-year-old children should spend more time playing with manipulatives than practicing writing skills. Some schools and/or families may push for children to begin formal handwriting before the children are developmentally ready to participate in this activity. If families or educational programs push young children to write before their hands are physically ready, it may have a negative impact on the children's interest in writing. In addition, preschoolers who have yet to develop the precursors for higher-level fine motor skills are at risk for developing poor pencil grasp, illegible handwriting, and slow handwriting (Benbow, 1990; Bredekamp & Copple, 2009; Case-Smith & Pehoski, 1992; Exner, 2005).

Preschoolers should be adept at several basic fine motor skills before they attempt more challenging activities like pre-writing and using scissors. Here is a list of the foundations of basic fine motor skills:

Developmental Readiness: Building, stacking, and putting things together all fascinate young children. Preschoolers begin to understand shapes and sizes and begin to differentiate between the "part" and the "whole." For instance, when you give a child a basket of play fruit that contains all apples and one banana, the child can recognize that the banana is not the same, even though it is one "part" of the "whole" fruit basket. Activities that give children the opportunity to build and construct using blocks and other similar objects also help them become developmentally ready to participate in activities such as drawing, cutting, and stringing beads.

Good Posture/Balance: Fine motor activities are easier to complete when a child sits with her feet firmly on the floor and with her back straight. A child should be able to give her full attention to her fine motor task rather than worrying about falling off her chair. The child should be able to use her arms to manipulate objects rather than using her arms to hold herself steady at the table.

Shoulder Strength: A child's shoulder strength provides her with a stable base of support for her hand function. Young children who do not regularly participate in large motor activities such as climbing, crawling, pushing, and pulling may not develop good upper-body strength. When these children attempt fine motor activities, their arms and hands may be shaky and uncoordinated because they are unable to hold their shoulders steady and in alignment.

Grasp: A child should be able to hold a writing tool (for example, a crayon, marker, or pencil) before pre-writing skills can develop. The grasp should be strong enough to hold the writing tool, but flexible enough to allow the child to move the tool across the paper. The strength and quality of a child's grasp will develop over time. While most three-year-olds hold a crayon with all of their fingers, the majority of five-year-olds use their thumb, index, and middle fingers to hold the crayon. Most typically developing children will have a mature grasp of a writing tool by the time they reach first grade.

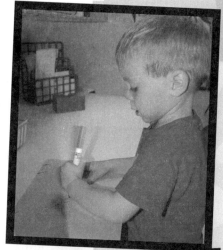

Forearm and Wrist Control: To effectively participate in fine motor activities, a child should be able to swivel her forearm so that her palm is up and then down. A child's ability to hold her wrist firm while moving her fingers is particularly important for activities such as cutting and lacing or stringing. These skills improve dramatically between the ages of three and five years.

Bilateral Hand Use: Using two hands together to complete an activity is essential for successful participation in fine motor activities. By age three, a child should be able to stabilize an object with one hand and move her other hand. For example, she should be able to hold down a piece of paper with one hand while drawing on that paper with her other hand. By age five, a child should begin developing **reciprocal hand use** where she can cut with one hand and turn the paper with the other hand to create large, simple shapes.

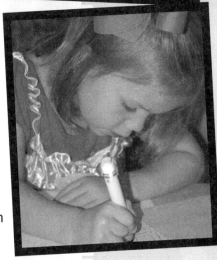

Eye-Hand Coordination: Effective interaction between visual and hand skills is important. The child needs to be able to use vision to coordinate the movement of her shoulders, elbows, wrists, and fingers as she learns to use a new tool or participates in a new fine motor activity. (Case-Smith & Pehoski, 1992; Klein, 1996)

This book includes activities that facilitate the development of these fundamental fine motor skills for three- and four-year-olds. Many five-year-olds have achieved adequate skills in these fundamental areas; therefore, a majority of the activities for five-year-olds address the fine motor skills of writing and manipulating small objects with two hands.

Development of Pre-Writing and Pre-Scissor Skills

As with all other motor skills, a developmental progression of pre-writing and pre-scissor-use skills exists. Each component of pre-writing and pre-scissor use builds upon the previous skill. Acquiring these skills will help young children to develop mature scissor and handwriting skills in the elementary grades (Exner, 2005; Klein, 1990).

Sequence of Pre-Writing

In addition to the precursors of effective fine motor skills described here, a young child must be able to scribble independently on paper before beginning pre-writing activities. The developmental stages of pre-writing include the abilities to:

- Copy a horizontal line.
- Copy a vertical line.
- Copy a circle.
- Copy a cross.
- Copy a right-to-left diagonal.
- Copy a square.
- Copy a left-to-right diagonal.
- Copy an "X."
- Copy a triangle.
- Copy a diamond.

Note: *"Copy" here means that the child can look at a picture or drawing of a particular form, and without a demonstration of how to make the line or shape, be able to create an imitation of the drawing.*

In general, the pre-writing sequence begins sometime around age two. Most children will be able to copy a triangle and a diamond by the time they are four-and-a-half years old. Once a child can copy all forms and shapes, that child should be ready to begin writing letters (Beery, 1997; Gardner, 1996; Klein, 1996; Weil & Amundson, 1994).

Developmentally appropriate preschool programs offer children various opportunities and materials with which to explore copying forms and shapes. The most effective fine motor activities are those that allow a young child to explore her own interests at her own pace. Best practice for young children does not include using worksheets to copy forms repetitively (Bredekamp & Copple, 1997).

Sequence of Pre-Scissor Use

A young child with well-developed scissor skills should be able to hold a piece of paper with one hand and use scissors in the other to cut the paper. The developmental stages of pre-scissor use that lead to well-developed scissor skills include the abilities to:

- Hold scissors appropriately (one hand, thumb on top).
- Open and close scissors.
- Snip paper.
- Cut forward through a sheet of paper.
- Cut in a straight line.
- Cut out a square or triangle.
- Cut out a circle.
- Cut non-paper material (such as yarn, tape, or fabric).

Note: *A child begins by cutting large simple shapes and progresses to cutting smaller shapes.*

The pre-scissor skills sequence typically begins when children are about two-and-a-half years old. Many young children first attempt to hold scissors with their thumbs down or using two hands.

By age three, a preschooler should be able to hold a sheet of paper in one hand and manipulate the scissors in her other hand well enough that she can snip the paper. By age five-and-a-half, most children can cut out simple shapes and use scissors to cut non-paper materials for creative activities.

These descriptions of how children develop their pre-writing and pre-scissor-use skills are guidelines, not rules. Each child will have her own interests and skill level. As a result, preschoolers will progress through the sequence differently as they develop these fine motor skills.

Chapter 2 addresses the impact of the learning environment on young children's ability to develop fine motor skills. The chapter describes a fine motor center and includes suggestions for layout, materials, and props. The chapter also describes the role of the teacher in guiding preschoolers' fine motor skills, giving careful consideration to the developmental sequence of learning. In addition, the chapter focuses on selecting tools and materials to best meet preschoolers' fine motor needs.

Chapter 2

Getting Started: The Importance of the Environment

Between infancy and age seven, young children develop more fine motor skills than at any other period in their lives. The preschool years are an especially explosive time for motor development. It is vital that preschoolers spend time in well-designed learning environments that offer ample opportunities for exploration and play. In the preschool classroom, children interact with teachers, peers, objects, and materials. Each interaction contributes to the development of a young child's fine motor skills.

It is impossible to overstate the role of the teacher in a child's fine motor development. A responsive and caring teacher helps establish a preschooler's sense of trust and security, and a child who feels nurtured and supported is more likely to try new things. Teachers should be careful observers of young children, in addition to being knowledgeable about typical preschool fine motor development. A knowledgeable teacher can watch a young child play and then join in to scaffold the child's development in new directions. Teachers can also select materials, tools, and activities that will best stimulate preschoolers' fine motor skills in enjoyable and developmentally appropriate ways.

How to Guide Pre-Writing Skills

Handwriting is an important life skill that the majority of young children begin learning during the preschool years. However, it is important not to push children to participate in writing activities that are physically, cognitively, and perceptually too challenging for them. If a child feels unsuccessful, he may lose interest in writing or develop poor handwriting habits that will follow him throughout his life. Young children who are not developmentally ready to begin writing are especially at risk to develop poor pencil grip and illegible handwriting.

Children learn pre-writing skills best by participating in play and daily life activities (Benbow, 1990; Case-Smith & Pehoski, 1992; Exner, 2005). With knowledge of the developmental steps that children typically follow in learning to write, teachers can help ensure that each preschooler will advance through the appropriate stages of pre-writing development.

Developmental Steps for Learning Pre-Writing

Modeling/Imitating: An adult or peer shows the child how to draw a line or shape. The child imitates it.
Tracing: The child traces over a line or shape. Some children are able to skip the tracing step, as they will be able to copy a shape after modeling/imitating.
Copying: The child looks at the completed line or shape and copies it.
Creating: The child creates his own lines and shapes.

The time that a child spends at each developmental step depends on many factors. Each time a child attempts a new form or shape, he will most likely need to go through these same steps. Expose young children to a wide variety of print, art, and writing tools during play so that the children have many opportunities to imitate and model pre-writing and can make the early connections necessary to begin writing.

By four years of age, many children will spend more time creating shapes and drawings of their own and less time imitating and tracing. During this stage, engaging in open-ended activities that use blank paper and various writing tools will allow a child to practice his new pre-writing skills. Teachers may transcribe young children's dictated ideas onto paper. Labeling a child's drawing, or writing his story on paper is a great way to demonstrate letter formation.

Some children are ready to begin writing at age five. Most children will start by writing their first names. Some children will be interested in writing letters that are not in their names and may begin to participate in inventive spelling. Young children should have many opportunities to express themselves on paper. Journaling or book-making may be effective activities for early writers (*Early Childhood Today*, 1998). The best way to promote a child's handwriting skills is to provide a literacy-rich environment that includes a variety of opportunities for the young child to observe, attempt, and master pre-writing activities first and then follow with letter writing activities (Exner, 2005; Klein, 1996; Weil & Amundson, 1994).

Hands at Play

To encourage the skills necessary for children to develop fine motor function, preschool classrooms need a large assortment of materials and objects that the children can manipulate with their hands. Most preschoolers enjoy using their hands to make creations with materials like beads, glue, paper, paint, and yarn. They also like using tools such as scissors, markers, pencils, paintbrushes, toy hammers, and screwdrivers. These manipulatives must be safe and easy for children to use.

When you give a child a new tool or material, first allow him some time to explore the object at his own pace. This type of play may include feeling, banging, or moving the object or materials in a repetitive manner. After the child finishes exploring the new object, demonstrate the proper way to use it. Then the child can progress to attempting to use the tool in its "real" manner. During this stage of symbolic representation where the child draws or constructs something that represents an object (for example, a child may draw a picture of

herself that may not resemble her closely) the preschooler may enjoy practicing the same method repeatedly. In the last stage of play, the young child should begin to exhibit some confidence in his ability to use the new object, and may branch out into new and unusual ways of playing with it.

Using Learning Centers to Encourage Fine Motor Development

A learning center provides an open-ended environment in which young children can explore and participate in various activities at their own interest levels. In this type of environment, a preschooler will be more willing to try new things and expand his learning potential. Because children learn fine motor skills best during play, centers that provide unique and appropriate tools and play materials work well in a preschool classroom (Parham & Fazio, 2007).

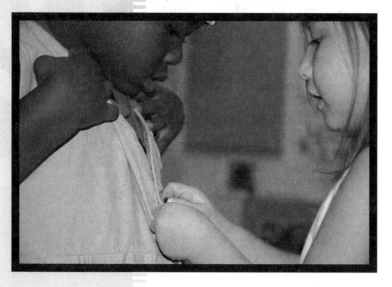

Traditional centers, such as the Block Center, Sand and Water Center, Art Center, and Home Living Center offer many opportunities for preschoolers to practice fine motor activities. For instance, dress-up clothes in the Home Living Center give children practice using zippers, snaps, buttons, Velcro, and laces. In the Block Center, offer small building blocks, miniature Lego blocks, or small magnetic blocks and pieces for children to use to stack and build.

Socio-dramatic centers present fine motor activities in a real-life setting and help children transfer the skills they develop there into new environments like the home and community. For example, in a Bakery and Cooking Center, preschoolers can practice rolling out, pinching, and cutting dough. Children in the Greenhouse Center can paint a flower pot, plant, water seeds, and chart plant growth. In a Restaurant Center, preschoolers can design menus, write customer orders, and create place mats for the tables (Isbell & Isbell, 2005; Isbell, 2008).

Fine Motor Center

A Fine Motor Center offers preschoolers the opportunity to observe and practice fine motor activities with their peers. The Fine Motor Center should be in a central location. In this center, children can work on many learning objectives, including developing pre-writing skills, improving bilateral hand (two-hand) use, expanding their scissor skills, and practicing eye-hand coordination. In the Fine Motor Center, preschoolers can experiment with a variety of tools and materials and gain confidence in completing fine motor tasks.

A Fine Motor Center should be available in the preschool classroom throughout the year. Set up and use the fine motor activities from this book in a center where you can observe how the children use tools and materials in their fine motor play. If the children become disinterested in the setup of the Fine Motor Center, consider adding new tools or materials to stimulate their curiosity in different ways. Rotating items in and out of the Fine Motor Center (or any center) is a good way to maintain young children's interest.

Layout of the Fine Motor Center

The Fine Motor Center will work best in a spot where the floors are easy to clean. If your entire floor is carpeted, cover the floor with a shower curtain or dropcloth to protect surfaces. The center must include the following items:

Tables and Chairs—It is important that preschoolers have work spaces that allow them to develop good posture and balance while engaging in different fine motor activities. Sturdy tables and chairs at an appropriate height are very important. Chairs should allow the young child's knees to bend at a 90° angle. Children sitting in the chairs should be able to place their feet firmly on the ground, rather than have their feet dangling in the air. The table should be a height that allows the child's elbows to bend and rest lightly on the tabletop. A table that is too low will cause a child to bend over his work, while a table that is too high can inhibit the child's hand function. Adjustable-height tables and chairs work best when trying to meet the sizing needs of individual children. However, placing telephone books or boxes under a child's feet is a simple way to provide a child with the necessary balancing support. Standing at a table is another good way for a child to develop his sense of balance as he completes various fine motor activities.

Vertical Surfaces—Writing on vertical surfaces—such as an easel, a wall-mounted dry-erase board, or a wall-mounted chalkboard—helps a child develop a good grasp and learn the appropriate wrist position for drawing and writing. Three-year-olds should draw or paint on a vertical surface every day. Drawing on a vertical surface tends to encourage the proper formation of shapes and letters.

Easels—Provide sturdy 3" three-ring binders the children can use as table-top easels (see instructions on page 82). Also consider taping or clipping paper to the wall to create a vertical drawing and writing surface. A Plexiglas Art Wall provides an easy-to-clean vertical surface for painting or drawing activities.

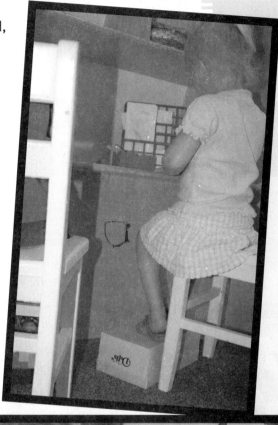

Plexiglas Art Wall

Materials

⅛" Plexiglas (cut to a size that fits your wall space)
4–8 screws or clips
tape or molding
screwdriver
shower curtain or drop cloth

Procedure

1. Screw Plexiglas securely into the wall at the preschoolers' eye level.
2. Cover the edges of the Plexiglas and screws with tape or molding.
3. Cover the floor with a shower curtain or drop-cloth.
Note: *You can use a squeegee to clean paint off the wall.*

Props for the Fine Motor Center

- Individual or large chalk board and eraser
- Large and small sticks of chalk
- Child-safe scissors
- Clay and/or playdough
- Dressing dolls with buttons, snaps, and zippers
- Easel
- Finger puppets
- Glue sticks and school glue
- Individual-size, dry-erase boards and washable, dry-erase markers
- Items for gluing (such as scrap paper, construction paper, tissue paper, craft sticks, straws, and fabric)
- Lacing cards/boards and laces
- Laminated paper for pre-writing and/or letter tracing
- Materials to paint, draw, and write on (construction paper, newsprint, white paper, bubble wrap, foil, wrapping paper, and so on)
- Materials for stringing (large and small beads, string, yarn, shoelaces, and thin rope) **Safety Note:** Always supervise young children when using these materials.
- Nuts, bolts, and screws of various sizes **Safety Note:** Always supervise young children when using these materials.
- Pegboards and pegs
- Puzzles (some with knobs)
- Rubber stamps and stamp pads
- Stickers
- Tongs of various sizes
- Tools for painting (large and very small paintbrushes, cotton balls, feathers, turkey baster, paint rollers, and sponges)
- Writing utensils, such as large and small crayons, pencils (adult-size and golf-size), chalk (large and small) and washable markers (thin and fat)
- Small, clear containers to hold items. Mark the containers with picture and word labels so children can quickly and accurately choose the tools and materials they want to use.

Just the "Write" Size: Selecting Tools and Materials

When implementing fine motor activities in a preschool setting, it is crucial to select tools and materials that are developmentally appropriate for young children. It is also a good idea to use materials that are both cost effective and environmentally friendly, such as old newspaper, magazines, and greeting cards. Preschoolers work best with tools that fit easily into their small hands. Select tools that will make it easy for a child to be successful. With the appropriate tools and materials, young children are more likely to develop self-confidence and a sense of pride about achieving independence in the particular fine motor activity.

Here are some suggestions of developmentally appropriate items to use during fine motor activities:

Writing and Drawing Utensils: The grasp that a child uses with a writing utensil is important because it has an effect on the child's handwriting. By the end of kindergarten, most children will have established a particular method for grasping their writing tools. These grasps are habit-based and are very difficult to change, once established. Using the appropriate size and type of writing utensil will help a young child develop and practice an efficient pencil grasp that will carry over into elementary school.

For younger and inexperienced preschoolers, provide large writing tools, such as thick chalk, pencils, crayons, and paintbrushes; bulb paintbrushes; and easy-grip (round-top) crayons. These "thick" utensils are easier for children to grasp in their small hands. Large markers are especially effective for beginning writers because large markers move smoothly across the paper and are easy to hold.

Some four-year-olds and most five-year-olds have developed enough skills for writing that they are ready to use standard-sized writing utensils. Adult-sized pencils, golf pencils, thin markers, and small paintbrushes will encourage a more efficient grasp. This means children will start to hold the writing tool with fewer fingers, as well as start to separate their thumb and index finger while writing. Do not throw away short pencils and broken crayons; keep them available to help the more mature preschooler learn to use his thumb, index, and middle finger to grasp a pencil.

Scissors: Small, round-tipped scissors are typically the best choice for preschoolers. Select scissors that have small holes for a young child's fingers and that are not longer than 5". School-style scissors, which both right- or left-handed children can use, work well. Make sure that the scissors are sharp enough to cut paper easily and that they open and close smoothly.

Cutting Materials: For beginning or less-skilled cutters, use heavyweight paper, such as oaktag, index cards, magazine inserts or junk-mail cards, construction paper, or paper bags. Heavier paper is less floppy, more stable, and will allow the child more control for cutting. Playdough is another heavy material that works well for snipping with scissors. Preschoolers with a moderate skill level can cut regular-weight paper. More advanced preschoolers may cut light-weight materials, such as foil, wax paper, and tissue paper. Non-paper items, such as yarn and fabric, are the most challenging to cut—save these until the child is skilled at cutting regular paper.

Glue: Glue sticks are valuable tools for preschoolers. They are easier to use than squeeze-bottle glue. Large glue sticks are preferable for young preschoolers. More experienced preschoolers can use smaller glue sticks that can apply glue to surfaces more accurately. Dipping craft sticks or cotton swabs into a small container of glue (for example, a small paper cup) may be useful for some activities. Once a preschooler develops enough hand strength to squeeze with control, he can begin to use school glue bottles in fine motor activities, as such bottles are also a great way for the child to build hand strength.

Stringing/Lacing: Stringing and lacing activities require good eye-hand coordination. Typically, young children learn to string objects first. Once they are confident in their stringing abilities, they will be more willing to attempt lacing activities, such as lacing cards or boards. When selecting materials for stringing or lacing, consider the size of the holes in the object, and the length of the hard tip of the string or lace. For young preschoolers, it helps to start stringing objects that have large holes and that the children can hold easily. String that is stiff and has a long, hard tip will be easier for small hands to manipulate. Rope with duct tape stabilizing the end, thick shoelaces, or long straws also work well. As a young child develops more skill, he can begin stringing very small objects, such as small jewelry beads, onto plastic string or thread. **Note**: Supervise children closely when using these materials.

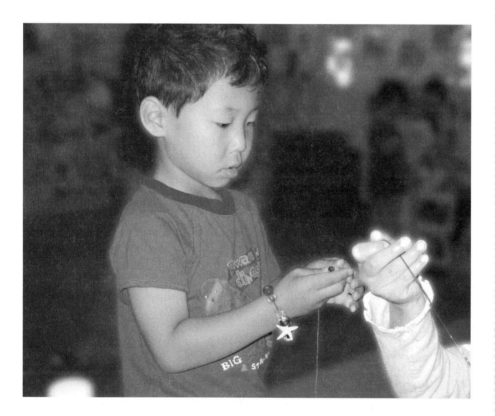

Chapters 3, 4, and 5 include fine motor activities that are specifically designed to address the developmental needs of three-year-olds, four-year-olds, and five-year-olds. The activities are easy to implement in preschool classrooms, and support young children's achievement of state standards for fine motor development in an effective and developmentally appropriate manner.

Chapter 3

Fine Motor Activities for Three-Year-Olds

What Can Most Three-Year-Old Children Do with Their Hands?

Three-year-old children are growing and developing at a rapid rate. During this period, their fine motor skills need to be nurtured in developmentally appropriate ways. Providing activities that allow children to build strength in their upper body, refine their grasp, and mature in their use of two hands together (bilateral hand skills) will establish the foundation for more expansive fine motor skills that will be explored in four-year-old and Pre-K classrooms.

Typical fine motor development covers a broad range of skills and abilities. Each child will develop at her own pace. Three-year-old children commonly demonstrate the following fine motor skills, which are not listed in a specific developmental sequence. Use these fine motor milestones as guidelines only, as you observe and teach young children.

- Copies a circle
- Imitates an accurate cross
- Threads large beads
- Builds a tower of 10 1" blocks
- Tears paper
- Cuts on a straight line
- Builds a train with blocks (one block on top and long line behind)
- Imitates a square
- Draws and paints with variety of large tools (for example, paint brushes, markers)
- Puts together simple, three- to four-piece puzzles
- Uses glue (with supervision) in projects
- Unbuttons large buttons
- Unzips zipper
- Feeds self well using spoon and fork
- Uses a digital pronate grasp (held with fingers; wrist straight; forearm moves with hand) OR a static tripod posture (held with thumb, index and middle fingers in crude manner; ring and pinky fingers are slightly bent; held high up on pencil)

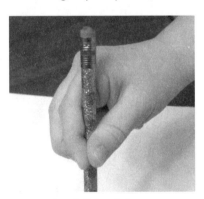

Static Tripod Grasp

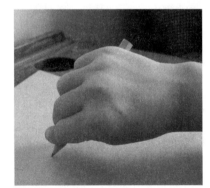

Digital Pronate Grasp

The activities in this chapter are especially designed to build the foundations for the fine motor development (see Chapter 1) of three-year-olds. Each activity focuses on at least one dimension of fine motor skills, such as upper-body strength, grasp of objects, or using two hands together. These activities have easy-to-follow directions and use simple materials and tools that are commonly found in developmentally appropriate preschool classrooms. Three-year-old children who participate in these activities will develop confidence in their ability to use their hands and will be better equipped when they advance to the next stage of fine motor development.

BILATERAL HAND SKILLS

Marble Painting

Objectives

The child will develop the ability to use two hands together (**bilateral hand skills**).

The child will improve **eye-hand coordination**.

Materials

9" pan or small box without lid

marble

paper

paint

spoon

Procedure

- Cut paper to fit the pan, and then line the bottom of the pan with paper.
- Ask the child to dip a marble into paint with a spoon and then place the marble inside the pan.
- Encourage the child to hold the pan with two hands and maneuver it so the marble rolls the paint onto the paper in an interesting pattern.
- She can continue to dip the marble in the paint and create designs as long as she is interested. Invite her to try using different colors of paint.

More Ideas

- Experiment with different-sized marbles and different types of paper.
- Ask the child if she can maneuver the pan so that the painted marble leaves a big circle on the paper.

Terms in bold are defined in the glossary, which begins on page 135

BILATERAL HAND SKILLS
Moving Bubbles

Objectives

The child will develop the ability to use two hands together.

The child will pour liquids.

Materials

clear, plastic lids of pie shells

measuring cups or other plastic cups for pouring

water

oil

food coloring

Procedure

- Give the child a clear, plastic pie-shell lid, and help her use the measuring cup to pour equal parts of water and oil into the plastic lid. The two liquids should just cover the bottom of the lid.
- Invite the child to select some food coloring and help her drip four or five drops of the food coloring around the plastic lid.
- Ask the child to hold the edges of the "plate" carefully with both hands and move it slowly from side to side.
- Observe how the colorful bubbles move around the "plate."

Another Idea

- Place the "plate" on an overhead projector or light table so that the light comes through and watch the colors move.

BILATERAL HAND SKILLS
Toy Workshop

Objectives

The child will increase hand strength.

The child will develop **bilateral hand skills**.

The child will participate in construction activity.

Materials

tools, such as toy hammers, screwdrivers, and mallets

large nuts and bolts that fit together

small pieces of PVC pipe and connectors

heavy-duty plastic or wooden toys

broken toys

Procedure

- Provide a variety of tools to use in the Toy Workshop.
- Show the child how to use the tools, as well as how to put various materials like nuts and bolts together.
- Encourage the child to build new toys or "repair" broken toys.
- Observe how the child uses the tools and materials in play.

Another Idea

- Add an empty toolbox to give the child more opportunities to sort tools and materials.

BILATERAL HAND SKILLS
Twinkle, Twinkle, Little Star

Objectives
The child will learn to coordinate two hands together.
The child will practice isolating finger movements.

Materials
recording of "Twinkle, Twinkle, Little Star" (optional)

Procedure
- Sing or play a recording of "Twinkle, Twinkle, Little Star."
- Use the illustrations to demonstrate the American Sign Language signs that correspond with the spoken words.
- Repeat the song, encouraging the children to sing and sign the song.

twinkle

little

More Ideas
- Show the child a picture of a star or a photograph of stars. Encourage the child to draw her own stars. **Note:** Many young children will not be able to draw a shape that resembles a star; their "stars" will likely be all shapes and sizes, which is developmentally appropriate.

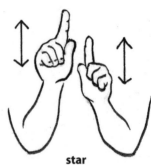

star

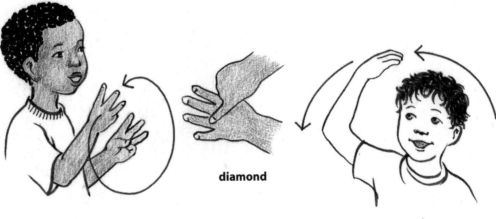

world

diamond

sky

DRAWING

Floor Drawing

Objectives

The child will develop the foundations for fine motor skills.

The child will gain upper-body strength.

The child will participate in drawing activities.

Materials

large sheets of paper

tape (recommended)

variety of drawing tools, such as large markers, crayons, or paintbrushes

Procedure

- Clear some open floor space for this activity. If using a carpeted area, provide a clipboard, a length of cardboard, or some other hard material that will make a firm surface on which to draw.
- Place the paper on the floor. Consider taping the paper to the floor to keep it secure.
- Provide markers, crayons, and other drawing tools.
- Invite the child to lie on her stomach to do Floor Drawings.

More Ideas

- Offer small pillows or blankets for the child to place under her elbows to keep her comfortable on the hard floor.
- This is a great activity to try outdoors; it can inspire the child to draw pictures of nature.

EYE-HAND COORDINATION

Styrofoam Construction

Objectives

The child will gain finger strength.

The child will expand tool usage.

The child will explore new building materials.

Materials

chunks of Styrofoam

duct or packing tape

golf tees

toy hammers or small mallets

Procedure

- To control a potentially messy situation, cover the outside edges of Styrofoam with tape.
- Place pieces of Styrofoam, golf tees, and hammers on the floor or a table.
- Discuss the appropriate and safe use of hammers and golf tees.
- Encourage the child to make a construction with the Styrofoam and golf tees.
- Demonstrate how the child can push golf tees into the Styrofoam with her fingers and with the hammer.
  Safety Note: Always observe closely to ensure the children use the hammer and golf tees safely.

More Ideas

- Add large markers to the Styrofoam construction materials so the child can decorate her building with markers.
- Challenge the child to construct tall Styrofoam buildings.

GRASP
Corn Picking

Objectives

The child will enhance **pincer grasp**.

The child will improve **eye-hand coordination**.

Materials

Indian corn

sand and water table or large plastic container full of sand

sand toys, such as small buckets and shovels, plastic spoons, and large funnels

Procedure

- Place several ears of Indian corn in the sand table or plastic container.
- Invite the child to "pick" the corn kernels off the ears and put them into the sand table or the container.
- Once she removes all of the corn kernels, she can explore this new material in the sand table.

Another Idea

- Add small plastic bottles, such as medicine bottles or travel-size bottles, to the sand table. The child can fill the bottles with kernels of corn and use them as shakers.

GRASP

Squeezy Water Play

Objectives

The child will improve grasp strength.

The child will develop foundations for fine motor skills.

The child will gain experience with new tools.

Materials

turkey basters

eyedroppers or pipettes

sponges in a variety of sizes, such as makeup sponges, kitchen sponges, natural
sponges, or large cleaning sponges

water table or large plastic container with water

plastic cups, bottles, and kitchen utensils

Procedure

- Show the child how to fill turkey basters, eyedroppers, and sponges with
  water.
- Observe ways that the child uses her new tools in play.
- Encourage the child to squeeze water from the tools to fill up cups or bottles.

More Ideas

- Add liquid soap to the water to add a new dimension to the activity.
- To promote pincer grasp, cut some sponges into small 1"–2" pieces.

GRASP

Stamp Art

Objectives

The child will improve grasp of small objects.

The child will increase finger strength.

Materials

paper

variety of stamps with small handles

washable inkpads

large washable markers

Procedure

● Provide paper, stamps, and markers for the child.

● Demonstrate how to use a marker to color the stamp rather than using the ink pad.

● Invite the child to explore different methods of using stamps to make art.

● Talk with the child about her Stamp Art creation.

Another Idea

● Make soap stamps by cutting small pieces of soap in half and carving out shapes or designs (adult only). Ink adheres to most soap, but Ivory® soap works well.

GRASP
Vertical Board Play

Objectives
The child will refine grasp.
The child will develop proper forearm posture and wrist positioning.

Materials
felt board and small felt pieces
magnetic board and small magnetic pieces such as shapes, animals, or letters
easel with tray (or use a wall)

Procedure
● Place the magnetic board or felt board in a vertical position by putting it on an easel or propping it securely against a wall. This will encourage the child to develop appropriate forearm and wrist positioning and grasp.
● Encourage the child to play with the magnetic pieces on the vertical board.
● Talk to the child about what she is creating with the felt or magnetic pieces.

More Ideas
● Read a story and ask the child to pick appropriate pieces and use them to re-enact the story on the vertical board.
● Encourage the child to sort the pieces by color or shape.

GRASP AND RELEASE

Mini-Muffin Sorting

Objectives

The child will improve grasp of small objects.

The child will sort objects.

The child will practice **eye-hand coordination**.

Materials

mini-muffin pans

small items to sort, such as buttons, tiny pegs, stones, marbles, coins, or
    paper clips

Procedure

- Give the child a mini-muffin pan.
- Set out the various small items and challenge the child to sort the items into matching groups (for example, putting all marbles together).

More Ideas

- Sort the objects using other criteria, such as color or shape.
- Help the child count the number of objects in each cup.

Great for Groups

HAND STRENGTH
Hide-and-Seek Playdough

Objectives
The children will develop hand strength.
The children will improve finger coordination.

Materials
playdough
small objects, such as marbles, coins, pegs,
    or plastic animals

Procedure
- This is a good activity to do with two or more children.
- Set out the playdough and small objects for the children to explore.
- Suggest that one child "hide" some of the objects inside the playdough.
- Ask another child to "find" the objects that the first child hid.
- Help the children take turns hiding the objects and finding them.

More Ideas
- Place small cups at the table. Ask the children to place each object they find inside the playdough into a small cup. Then help the children count how many objects they found.

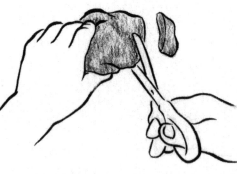

- Ask the children to close their eyes and try to find the objects hidden in the playdough using only their fingers.
- Cutting playdough improves hand strength, so provide child-safe scissors and encourage the children to cut the playdough into pieces.

HAND STRENGTH
Sand Castle Clay

Objectives

The child will improve hand strength.

The child will enhance fine motor coordination.

The child will make new creations with her hands.

Materials

large bowl and a spoon for mixing (**Note:** Sand may scratch the bowl during mixing.)

1 cup sand

1 package Jell-O® sugar-free gelatin

½ cup cornstarch

¾ cup hot water

1 tsp alum (found in the spice aisle of your grocery store)

food coloring

Note: Double the recipe if you plan to do the activity listed below in "Another Idea."

Procedure

● Mix all the ingredients together in a large bowl (adult-only step).

● Allow the clay to cool (adult-only step), and then knead it.

● Encourage the child to mold sand castles with her hands.

● Observe how the child uses her hands to manipulate clay.

Another Idea

● Provide sand tools, such as small hand-held shovels, buckets, or craft sticks, and small shells for decorating castles.

"Pop" Straws

Objectives
The child will develop pre-scissor skills.
The child will gain confidence in using scissors.

Materials
plastic straws (must be thick plastic)
child-safe scissors

Procedure
- Show the child how to hold a straw with one hand and snip pieces from it with the scissors. Say "Pop!" as you cut the straw.
- Encourage the child to cut her straw and listen for the "pop!"

More Ideas
- Provide paper and glue for the child to make unusual artwork with her pieces of straw.
- Help the child stack or build "structures" with straw pieces and glue.
- Use the pieces of straw to string on thread as you would beads.

PRE-SCISSOR SKILLS
Card Cutting

Objectives
The child will practice holding scissors appropriately.
The child will gain control of scissors.

Materials
card-weight paper including magazine inserts, junk mailings, greeting cards, or
  index cards
child-safe scissors

Procedure
- Cut greeting cards into single pieces (instead of folded), so they are easier for children to manipulate.
- Demonstrate the proper way to hold and cut with scissors. Give the child verbal cues, such as "Thumb on top!" or "Open, close, open, close."
- Invite the child to cut the cards with scissors.
- Help the child to hold the scissors correctly, if necessary.

More Ideas
- Make a shaker out of scrap card pieces. Help the child cut her card into confetti. Place the confetti inside a clean, clear, dry plastic bottle. Secure the lid onto the bottle with glue.
- Use the pieces of card and paper the children produce as collage materials in art projects.

PRE-SCISSOR SKILLS
Clothespin Airplanes

Objectives
The child will develop the foundations of scissor skills.

The child will develop hand strength.

Materials
wooden clothespins (squeeze type)

craft sticks

glue (wood glue works best)

pizza boards or pieces of cardboard

Procedure
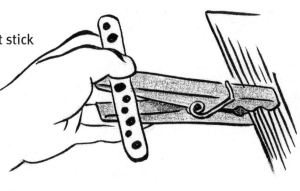

- Help the child glue a craft stick to one stem of the squeezable end of each clothespin. The craft stick should be perpendicular to the clothespin, similar to a tail wing for an airplane. Allow to dry thoroughly.
- Give the child a piece of cardboard to use as a runway.
- Show the child how to squeeze the clothespins with her fingers on the "tail wing" so that the airplane will open.
- The child can take the plane in for a landing by squeezing the clothespins to open them and then placing them around the edges of the cardboard as though they are "landing" on the runway.

More Ideas
- The child can use markers, paint, or glitter to decorate her airplanes or design her runways.
- Hang runways vertically at the child's shoulder height to add a new landing challenge.

PRE-SCISSOR SKILLS
Shredded Paper Collage

Objectives
The child will tear paper with two hands.

The child will develop eye-hand coordination.

The child will use glue to create art.

Materials
pieces of medium-weight paper, such as construction paper or paper bags

pieces of light-weight paper, such as newspaper or magazines

glue sticks or small bowls of glue

plain paper (to serve as the background of the collage)

Procedure
- Encourage the child to use two hands to tear strips of paper to make shredded paper.
- The child can tear small or long pieces of paper.
- Encourage the child to glue the shredded paper onto a clean piece of paper to make a collage. She may use glue sticks or dip the strips of paper into glue.
- Talk about the creation that the child made. Is the collage flat or raised? Are the shredded pieces of paper long or short?

More Ideas
- Invite the child to paint her shredded paper collage after the glue dries. This will add another dimension to the art.
- Sprinkle glitter on the collage while the glue is still wet.

PRE-SCISSOR SKILLS
Squirt Game

Objectives

The child will develop hand strength for scissor skills.

The child will improve **eye-hand coordination**.

Materials

small, plastic spray bottles filled with water

bath soap foam (color foam works best)

finger paint paper or wax paper

plastic shower curtain or sheet

easel or wall

Procedure

Note: This is a great outdoor activity.

● Cover floor with a shower curtain or sheet.

● At the child's shoulder level, clip or tape paper to an easel or the wall.

● Help child make a target by squirting bath soap foam in a circle (target shape) on the paper. Ask the child to squirt the target with water.

● See how many squirts it takes to wash the target away.

More Ideas

● Experiment with different sizes of targets.

● Experiment with standing a different distance away from the target.

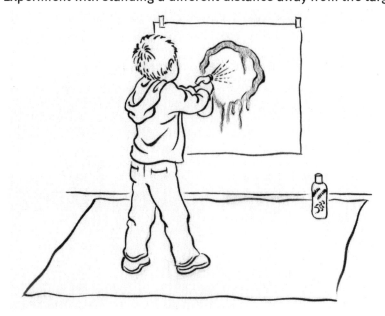

PRE-SCISSOR SKILLS
Tong Pick-Up

Objectives

The child will practice opening and closing tools.

The child will build strength and coordination in hands.

Materials

variety of tongs (large, small, plastic, metal)

variety of tweezers (large, small, plastic, metal)

small objects, such as cotton balls, cotton swabs, pieces of sponge, crayons, small blocks, pegs, or Lego® blocks

variety of containers

Procedure

- Show the child how to use tongs and tweezers to pick up small objects.
- Encourage the child to use the tongs and tweezers to place objects into the various containers.
- Ask her which objects are easier and which objects are more difficult to pick up with the tools. Ask her which tool is the easiest to use and which is the hardest. Talk about why that might be so.

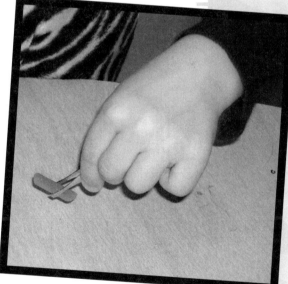

More Ideas

- Add playdough to the activity. The child can roll small balls, snakes, or tear the playdough into pieces to pick up with tongs or tweezers.
- See how many objects the child can put into a container without dropping one.

PRE-WRITING SKILLS
Body Shapes

Objectives

The child will improve **bilateral coordination**.

The child will identify shapes.

The child will develop pre-writing skills.

Materials

Procedure

- Show the child an example of a line (for example: vertical, horizontal, or diagonal) or shape (for example: circle, square, or triangle).

- Ask the child to use her body to form that line or shape.

- Observe how the child makes the shape.

- If the child is having difficulty, demonstrate how to make the line or shape with your body.

- With the child, talk about the characteristics of the shape. For instance, a circle is round like a wheel and a square has four sides.

- Encourage the child to try to make the shape again, and help her as needed.

More Ideas

- Take photographs of the child making the Body Shapes. Hang the photos alongside a drawing of the corresponding shape so the child has a model to look at later when trying to make the shape again.

PRE-WRITING SKILLS
Cardboard Stencils

Objectives
The child will gain experience drawing shapes.

The child will develop foundations for writing.

Materials
scrap pieces of cardboard (two-ply cardboard works well)

adult scissors or knife (for adult use only)

large markers or large crayons

paper

Procedure
- Cut out circles, squares, and triangles from cardboard (adult-only step). **Note:** Shapes that are 4"–6" in diameter work best for preschool-aged children. Save the outside pieces of cardboard to use as stencils.

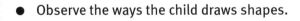

- Show the child how to use cardboard shapes and stencils for drawing and tracing. Encourage her to use one hand to hold the stencil and the other hand to trace around the edge.
- Observe the ways the child draws shapes.

More Ideas
- To encourage a good grasp and wrist posture, use clips to place stencils on an easel. This will give the child the experience of writing on a vertical surface.
- Invite the child to use card stock to create greeting cards and use the stencils to decorate them.

No-Mess Finger Painting

Objectives

The child will develop **finger isolation**.

The child will learn to make simple lines or shapes.

Materials

resealable plastic freezer bags, any size

fingerpaints

Procedure

- Give the child a resealable, plastic freezer bag.
- Allow the child to select a color of fingerpaint, and then help the child pour the fingerpaint into her bag.
- Help her close and seal the bag securely. Be sure to press out the excess air. Tape the bag closed for extra security.
- Place the sealed bag flat on the table or floor.
- Show the child how to use her index fingers to make lines or shapes in the paint.
- Talk about the different shapes or designs that the child makes.

More Ideas

- Squirt two different colors of paint into the bag. Encourage child to use her index finger to mix the paint together.
- Explore what new colors the child can create by mixing paint.

PRE-WRITING SKILLS

Racing Tracks

Objectives

The child will develop foundations for writing.

The child will trace lines and shapes.

Materials

large sheet of paper

paint, markers, or electrical tape

variety of small cars and trucks

Procedure

- Cut a sheet of paper large enough to cover the entire tabletop or floor space.
- Draw or use electrical tape to make a racetrack, using circles and large vertical, horizontal, and diagonal lines.

Note: Keep the pattern simple and make lines a solid color.

- Encourage the child to drive her cars and trucks on the racetrack.
- Ask the child to identify the round and straight lines of the track.

More Ideas

- Help the child design and draw her own tracks, by using a variety of lines and shapes.
- Encourage the child to dip the wheels of the cars into paint and then trace the lines and shapes of the tracks.

PRE-WRITING SKILLS

Wall Washing

Objectives

The child will develop the foundations for writing.

The child will draw lines and shapes.

Materials

sidewalk chalk

large adult-size paintbrushes (at least 3" wide) or paint rollers

large bucket of water

liquid soap (if you want to use soapy water)

sidewalk chalk

outside wall or fence

Procedure

- Show the child how to use sidewalk chalk to draw large circles, crosses, and horizontal, vertical, and diagonal lines on the outside wall or fence at the child's shoulder level or below.
- Provide the child with a bucket of water and paintbrushes or rollers.
- Ask the child to "wash the wall" with the paintbrushes or rollers.
- Demonstrate how to trace the lines or shapes with the wet paintbrush to make the drawing disappear.

Another Idea

- Use large sponges or rags instead of paintbrushes to wash the wall.

PRE-WRITING SKILLS
Yarn Shapes

Objectives
The child will trace simple shapes.

The child will use glue and other art materials in play.

Materials
paper with horizontal lines, vertical lines, circles, squares, and triangles drawn on it

markers

glue stick or cotton swabs

small bowl of glue

yarn pre-cut into various lengths

Procedure
- Give the child the paper with lines or shapes drawn on it.
- Ask the child to trace over the lines or shapes with glue.
- Encourage the child to glue yarn to the lines or shapes.
- Engage the child in a discussion about the shapes she made.
- Once the glue is dry, the child can feel and trace the yarn shapes with her fingers.

More Ideas
- Give the child a blank sheet of paper and invite her to make her own yarn lines or shapes.
- Use the completed yarn shapes as templates and encourage the child to trace inside or outside the shapes with markers.
- You can also use the completed sheet with the yarn shapes to make a simple crayon rubbing. Place a sheet of plain paper on top and rub back and forth with a crayon. See what happens!

Cup Tower

Objectives

The child will gain experience with lacing.

The child will develop eye-hand coordination.

The child will feel confident in lacing skills.

Materials

small paper cups, such as bathroom cups

coffee stirrers or plastic straws

pieces of Styrofoam

Procedure

- Poke a small hole in the bottom of each small paper drinking cup (adult-only step). Make sure the hole is just big enough for the straw or coffee stirrer.

- Encourage the child to use coffee stirrers or plastic straws to string the paper cups together.

- Show the child how to stick one end of the straw into a Styrofoam base, to make the cup tower stand tall.

- Talk to the child as she is creating the tower. Ask questions. For instance, ask, "How many cups did you use?" "Can you fit another one on?"

More Ideas

- If the child has difficulty holding or lacing the cups, consider having her place one end of the straw into the Styrofoam before beginning. This will hold the straw steady.

- Provide the child with markers so she can decorate the paper cups.

STRINGING / LACING
Ribbon Pull

Objectives
The child will participate in a pre-lacing activity.
The child will improve **pincer grasp**.

Materials
clean coffee can with plastic lid
variety of ribbons, in different colors and widths
scissors and sharp knife (for use by adults only)

Procedure
- Cut pieces of ribbon into different lengths at least 12" long (adult-only step).
- Use a knife to cut slits in the coffee can lid for each ribbon; thread ribbons through the slits (adult-only step).
- Tie a knot on one end of each ribbon. **Note:** The knot should be inside the can when you secure the lid.
- Position the ribbons so that a small piece of each one sticks out from the top of the lid.
- Secure the lid (adult-only step).
- Demonstrate how to pull each ribbon with your fingers.
- Invite the child to pull the ribbons. Once all the ribbons are as far out of the can as possible, remove the lid and reposition the ribbons to start again.

Another Idea
- Once all the ribbons are out, talk about the colors, textures, lengths, and widths. Help her determine which ribbon is the longest and which is the shortest.

Shish-Kabob Snack

Objectives

The child will participate in lacing activity.

The child will develop **bilateral hand skills.**

The child will improve **eye-hand coordination**.

Materials

foods that are easy to skewer, such as bananas, pineapple, strawberries, melon, and so on

wooden shish-kabob skewers or chopsticks

Procedure

- Give the child a wooden skewer or chopstick. **Safety Note:** Skewers have sharp ends, so be sure to supervise the child closely while she is handling the skewer.
- Invite the child to select food items. Encourage her to lace the food onto the skewer.
- Discuss with the child the shapes and colors of food items.
- After the child finishes making her shish-kabob snack, invite her to eat and enjoy it!

More Ideas

- Challenge the child to count how many pieces of food are on her skewer.
- Suggest that the child create a food pattern, such as banana, pineapple, banana, pineapple.

STRINGING/LACING
Straw Jewelry

Objectives

The child will develop self-confidence in stringing beads.

The child will participate in **eye-hand coordination** activity.

The child will improve **bilateral hand skills**.

Materials

colorful straws

child-safe scissors

plastic string for making jewelry

Procedure

● Invite the child to cut straws into small pieces, ½"–1" in length.

Note: See "Pop" Straws activity on page 44 for more ideas with straws.

● Help the child cut a piece of string long enough for a necklace or bracelet.

● Tie a large knot in one end of the string.

● Encourage the child to string pieces of straw onto the string.

● When the string is full of straw pieces, help the child tie the ends together to make a bracelet or necklace.

More Ideas

● See if the child can make a pattern by using different colors of straw pieces. Simple patterns, using two colors, will work best for three-year-olds.

Great for Groups

UPPER BODY STRENGTH
Walk Like an Animal

Objectives
The child will develop upper-body strength needed for fine motor activities.
The child will improve **bilateral coordination**.

Materials
none

Procedure
- This is a great activity to try either inside or outside, though it requires a certain amount of open floor space.
- Sing the song "This is the way we walk like a (*insert animal name*)" to the tune of "Here We Go 'Round the Mulberry Bush."
- Select animals that the child can imitate. Animals that require the child to place her hands or her body on the floor will build more strength in the upper body. Some suggestions include: bear, cat, dog, snake, frog, crab, and giraffe.
- Demonstrate how to "walk" like the animal.
- Encourage the child to move her body and pretend to be each animal.

More Ideas
- Ask the child to pick an animal and demonstrate how that animal walks.
- With the child, read a book about animals and talk about the ways the different animals in the book move.

Chapter 4

Fine Motor Activities for Four-Year-Olds

What Can Most Four-Year-Old Children Do With Their Hands?

Four-year-old children greatly expand their repertoire of fine motor skills. Most four-year-olds learn to use thin writing and drawing utensils to trace, copy, and form a variety of shapes. They also gain independence in simple scissor skills, such as cutting on a straight line. Children in this age range enjoy manipulating various materials such as clay, playdough, and sand during their play. They explore the use of new tools to create artwork. These experiences are necessary to prepare the four-year-old child's hands for more challenging fine motor activities.

Typical fine motor development covers a broad range of skills and abilities. Each child will develop at his own pace. Four-year-olds commonly demonstrate the following fine motor skills, which are not listed in a specific developmental sequence. Use these fine motor milestones as guidelines only, as you observe and work with young children.

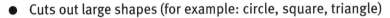

- Cuts out large shapes (for example: circle, square, triangle)
- Copies a square
- Copies a triangle
- Copies a cross
- Draws a person (may include a circle with two lines or be as detailed as a head, body, legs, arms and fingers)
- Makes marks to represent name
- Draws and paints with a variety of sizes and types of utensils (such as markers, paintbrushes, pencils, or crayons)
- Puts together simple puzzles
- Strings small beads
- Utilizes an easy-to-squeeze 1-hole punch and stapler, with close supervision
- Laces simple cards
- Manipulates clay or playdough with hands
- Uses tools such as a play hammer, rolling pin, or plastic knife with clay or playdough
- Uses fingers to act out simple fingerplays and songs
- Uses a zipper independently (may need help starting)
- Buttons large buttons
- Snaps easy snaps
- Pours liquid into cup
- Draws a picture that does not include all the characteristics of objects known to him (for instance, the child may draw a square for a car and leave out the wheels)
- Attempts to sign his name (although may often delete, reverse, inaccurately form letters, or write them from right to left)
- Uses a **static tripod grasp** (holding the writing tool with thumb, index, and middle fingers in crude manner; ring and pinky fingers are slightly bent; held high up on the pencil) or **dynamic tripod grasp** (holding the writing tool with tips of thumb, index, and middle fingers; ring and pinky fingers bent; hand moves separately from forearm)

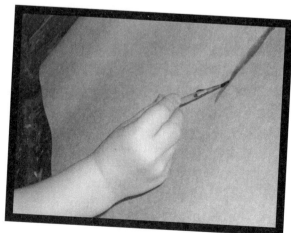

Dynamic Tripod Grasp

The activities in this chapter are designed specifically for use with four-year-old children, and they address a more challenging range of fine motor skills, such as refined grasp of utensils and coordination of two hands together. The activities will expand the four-year-old child's development of writing, drawing, cutting, and lacing skills. Children will also gain experience with new tools such as a 1-hole punch and mallet.

If you have four-year-olds who need more practice with fine motor skills, you may prefer to begin with some of the activities presented in Chapter 3, as it focuses on helping children build the foundation necessary for success in age-appropriate fine motor activities.

COLORING
Crayon Rubbings

Objectives

The child will participate in an art activity.

The child will improve **eye-hand coordination**.

Materials

large and/or small crayons with paper peeled off

white drawing paper

flat objects with texture, such as leaves and coins

templates of shapes, letters, or animals

Procedure

- Present the child with the various flat, textured objects and ask him to select an object.
- Ask the child to close his eyes and feel the object with his fingers.
- Show the child how to place the paper on top of the object and color over it.
- Observe how the child makes the crayon rubbings.
- Discuss the child's creations with him and label the objects he used to make them.

More Ideas

- Provide black paper and chalk with which the child can create more rubbings.
- Select new or unusual objects to use in crayon rubbings.
- Discuss questions that encourage imagination (for example, "What if the object isn't flat?" "What if the object doesn't have a texture?").

Terms in bold are defined in the glossary, which begins on page 135

EYE-HAND COORDINATION
Dressing Up

Objectives
The child will unzip and zip clothing.

The child will manipulate buttons and snaps.

The child will gain independence in dressing.

Materials
dress-up clothes with zippers

dress-up clothes with large buttons

dress-up clothes with simple snaps

Procedure
- Provide dress-up clothing that includes zippers, large buttons, and snaps.
- Demonstrate techniques for fastening zippers, buttons, and snaps.
- Encourage the child to try playing dress-up and using the fasteners himself.
- If the child is unable to begin fastening independently, start the process and allow him to finish. For example, help the child place the button inside the buttonhole and then allow the child to pull the button through. This technique will help the child develop confidence in his attempts at fastening.

Another Idea
- Using dolls or stuffed animals with fasteners on their clothing gives the child another opportunity to develop independence in dressing.

EYE-HAND COORDINATION

Finger Puppets

Objectives

The child will develop finger coordination.

The child will use individual fingers to express himself with puppets.

Materials

child-size gloves (small women's gloves may also work—shop for them at a thrift store)

scissors (adult-use only)

school glue or fabric glue in small bowls and cotton swabs (school glue will require more drying time)

markers

sequins, small buttons, small pom-poms, and plastic eyes

Procedure

- Cut the fingers out of gloves (adult-only step). You will use only the fingers of the gloves for this activity.
- Give the child at least two finger puppets to decorate.
- Provide markers, sequins, buttons, small pom-poms, and plastic eyes with which the child can decorate his finger puppet.
- After the glue on the finger puppets dries, invite the child to use his finger puppets to put on a show.
- Encourage the child to use puppets on both hands in his finger puppet show.

Another Idea

- Ask the child to act out a favorite story, book, or song with his finger puppets.

EYE-HAND COORDINATION
Photo Puzzles

Objectives
The children will put together simple puzzles.

The children will use various tools in play.

Materials
digital camera

printer

thick paper, such as card stock or oak tag

glue sticks

child-size scissors

small, resealable plastic freezer bags (to store the puzzles after use)

Procedure
- Use the digital camera to take a close-up photograph of the child or children.
- Print the photographs on 5" x 7" or 8" x 10" photo paper.
- Give each child a piece of card stock to fit his photograph (5" x 7" or 8" x 10").
- Ask the children to glue their photograph to the card stock and allow them to dry completely.
- Show the children how to cut the attached photographs into six or eight irregularly shaped puzzle pieces, assisting them, as needed.
- Encourage the children to take apart and put together their own puzzles. Invite the children to swap puzzles with other children.

Another Idea
- If a camera and printer are not available, use magazine photos instead.

GRASP

Cookie Decorating

Objectives

The child will refine grasp and release skills.

The child will build hand strength.

The child will express himself through fine motor skills.

Materials

sugar cookies

cake icing

edible sprinkles

tubes of decorating icing (squeeze type)

plastic knives and spoons

condiment cups

Procedure

- Spoon sprinkles and cake icing into nut cups so that each child has his own decorating materials.
- Encourage the child to spread icing onto cookies using knives or spoons. The child may use squeezable tubes of icing to decorate his cookies.
- Suggest that the child use his fingers to place sprinkles—one pinch at a time—on his cookies. Eat and enjoy!

More Ideas

- Provide toothpicks for drawing designs in the icing.

GRASP

Drops of Color

Objectives

The child will develop a grasp needed to hold tools.

The child will practice pre-scissor skills.

Materials

medicine droppers

food coloring

water

small bowl(s)

basket-type coffee filters

Procedure

- Mix food coloring with water in the bowl. You may prefer to use different colors in different bowls for this activity.
- Demonstrate the technique for filling up medicine droppers with water. Then, show the child how to squeeze the medicine dropper to make "drops of color" on the coffee filter.
- Invite the child to create his own "drops of color."

More Ideas

- The "drops of color" art makes a very interesting sun catcher. Help the child punch a hole in the top of the filter and tie on a piece of string. Hang the art in front of a window. **Note**: Laminate if desired.

GRASP
Reusable Stickers

Objectives

The child will improve his grasp of small objects.

The child will refine his release of small objects.

Materials

reusable stickers, such as Colorforms, Unisets, or window stickers

small dry-erase board or hand-held unbreakable mirror

easel or incline board (see Incline Writing Boards activity on page 82 for
   instructions)

Procedure

- Place a dry-erase board or mirror on an easel or incline board.
- Encourage the child to use stickers to decorate the board or tell a story.
- When the play is over, ask the child to remove stickers and replace them into
  storage.

More Ideas

- Provide dry-erase markers with which the child may trace around re-usable
  stickers.
- Consider having the child decorate a nearby window with stickers.

GRASP
Seed Art

Objectives

The child will develop pincer grasp.

The child will manipulate a variety of art materials.

Materials

variety of seeds, such as pumpkin, sunflower, or apple

glue

small bowls or nut cups

cotton swabs

construction paper

large markers

shape templates

Procedure

- Encourage the child to draw shapes on his construction paper. Alternately, he may use templates to trace shapes. **Note:** Do not cut out the shapes.

- Pour glue into small bowls, provide cotton swabs for dipping, and pour seeds into small bowls or nut cups (adult-only step).

- Show the child how to use the cotton swabs to dab glue onto his shapes, and invite him to place seeds on the glue, filling in the shape.

Another Idea

- Once the art dries, the child can use child-safe scissors to cut out the shapes.

GRASP
Stick Houses

Objectives
The child will use pincer grasp of small objects.
The child will develop **bilateral coordination**.

Materials
toothpicks
glue in small container for dipping
cotton swabs
thick paper, such as index cards, oak tag, or poster board

Procedure
- Give the child a piece of thick paper to use as the "foundation" for his construction.
- Demonstrate how to dip toothpicks into glue or use cotton swabs to place glue on a structure to hold it in place.
- Encourage the child to build houses with toothpicks.

Another Idea
- Read or tell the story of the "Three Little Pigs," and then encourage the child to try building with pieces of straw or craft sticks.

GRASP

Tape It Up!

Objectives

The child will experiment with tape.

The child will use materials for self expression.

The child will develop grasp strength.

Materials

masking tape

clear tape

variety of paper

child-safe scissors

paper towel rolls

Procedure

- Place the different tapes and a variety of papers on a table along with the paper towel rolls.
- Encourage the child to tape the paper to the paper towel roll to create original work.
- Show the child how to tear the tape.
- Observe how he uses the materials for self-expression.

Another Idea

- Ask the child to describe his creation. Transcribe his words, if he is interested. Display the description alongside the original work.

HAND STRENGTH
All-Terrain Vehicles

Objectives

The child will gain hand strength necessary for fine motor skills.

The child will practice directional terms needed for handwriting success.

Materials

sand table or large plastic container

various "terrains," including sand, potting soil, pebbles, pea gravel, and mulch

variety of very small toy trucks or construction vehicles

Procedure

- Prepare one "terrain" on each part of the table (For example: put sand at one end of the table and potting soil on the other end).
- Invite the child to drive his "All Terrain Vehicles" through/over the terrain.
- Propose building hills or mountains out of the material laid out on the table.
- Suggest that the child drive his vehicles "over," "around," and "through" the hills. Demonstrate these directions, as needed.

Another Idea

- Invite the child to use his vehicles to make different track shapes in the terrain.

HAND STRENGTH
More Peas Please

Objectives

The child will develop effective grasp of utensils.

The child will improve finger strength for fine motor skills.

Materials

green playdough

plastic bowls and spoons

Procedure

- Demonstrate how to use your thumb, index, and middle fingers to create "peas" by rolling playdough into small balls.
- Remind the child that the "peas" are pretend.
- Encourage the child to make tiny "peas" out of the playdough.
- Once the child masters the rolling motion, challenge him to use the spoon to fill bowls with "peas."

More Ideas

- Add plastic forks to the activity. See if the child can catch the peas on his fork.
- Encourage the child to use his index fingers to "smoosh" the peas.

Disappearing Holes

Objectives
The child will use a 1-hole punch
The child will gain experience cutting with scissors.
The child will improve **eye-hand coordination**.

Materials
polka-dot shapes (see Polka-Dot Shapes activity on page 95)
child-safe scissors

Procedure
- Make "polka-dot shapes." See Polka-Dot Shapes activity on page 95 for procedures. The child will have a sheet of paper on which punched holes form a shape (circle, square, triangle, and so on).

- Show the child how to use child-safe scissors to cut out the shape by cutting through the centers of the punched holes, The cut-out shapes will have scalloped edges when the child finishes cutting through the holes along the edges.
- Encourage the child to stay on the polka dots as he cuts out the shapes.
- Invite the child to feel and explore the edges of these new shapes.

Another Idea
- If the child isn't developmentally ready to cut out more elaborate shapes, use the 1-hole punch to form simple lines (horizontal, vertical, or diagonal) for him to cut.

PRE-SCISSOR SKILLS
Making a Wreath

Objectives

The child will develop scissor skills.

The child will use two hands to tear paper.

Materials

paper plates

glue sticks or small container of glue for dipping

colored tissue paper

child-safe scissors

Procedure

- Show the child how to fold a paper plate in half.
- The child should cut a semi-circle around the inside of the paper plate.
- Unfold the plate to reveal a "wreath."
- Encourage the child to tear small pieces of tissue paper and then use his fingers to squeeze the paper into balls.
- Provide a glue stick for the child to use to cover the "wreath" in glue, or dip each tissue paper ball into glue.
- Glue the tissue balls onto the wreath. When the glue dries, display the wreath prominently.

Another Idea

- Help the child punch two holes at the top of the wreath and lace yarn or ribbon through the holes so that he can hang the wreath. This makes a wonderful gift or room decoration.

PRE-SCISSOR SKILLS
Paper Chains

Objectives
The child will gain experience with scissors.

Materials
construction paper
child-safe scissors
glue sticks

Procedure
- Show the child how to cut strips of paper. Draw lines on paper for the child to follow, if needed.
- Ask the child to cut strips of construction paper.
- Show the child how to glue the ends of paper to form circles, and then how to link the circles together to make paper chains.

Another Idea
- Use the paper chains as decorations during holidays or for special occasions; or use them as measuring tools. For instance, the child can measure his height with the chains.

PRE-SCISSOR SKILLS
Place Mats

Objectives
The child will become more adept at using scissors.
The child will create art using a variety of materials.

Materials
construction paper or large, plain paper bags cut into rectangles
variety of writing utensils, such as crayons, markers, paint, and glitter glue
laminating materials or clear contact paper
child-safe scissors

Procedure
- Invite the child to decorate his paper place mat.
- Laminate the place mats (adult-only step).
- Demonstrate how to snip the edges of the paper to make a fringe.
- Encourage the child to use child-safe scissors to create a fringe around the outside edge of the paper.

More Ideas
- Invite the child to trace around a fork, spoon, and knife in their appropriate positions on the placemat. The child can use this place mat to help him remember how to set his place at the table.
- Laminated place mats make great gifts.

Feely Shapes

Objectives

The child will learn to draw shapes.

The child will use hands to manipulate small objects.

The child will participate in pre-writing activity.

Materials

variety of textured fabric, including velvet, faux fur,
    corduroy, denim, silk, and lace

adult scissors (fabric scissors work best)

cardboard, paper, and glue

writing and drawing tools

Procedure

- Cut pieces of cardboard into different shapes of various sizes from 2" across and larger. Cut matching shapes out of differently textured pieces of fabric. Glue the fabric to each shape and let the shapes dry (adult-only step).

- Encourage the child to explore the different textures of the "Feely Shapes."

- Talk with the child about the shapes and show how to trace around the "Feely Shapes."

More Ideas

- Cut out pieces of cardboard and allow the child to select his own fabric with which to cover the shapes. Cut the fabric to fit and help the child glue the fabric to the cardboard shapes.

- Place the "Feely Shapes" inside a bag or box. Ask the child to reach into the container and identify each shape by the way it feels. Ask questions to guide the child, such as, "Does it have sides? Is it round?"

PRE-WRITING SKILLS

Glue Shapes and Letters

Objectives

The child will trace shapes or letters.

The child will develop hand strength.

The child will control placement of glue.

Materials

color glue and/or glitter glue

paper

Procedure

- Draw shapes or write a child's name on paper.
- Demonstrate how to squeeze bottles to trace the shapes or letters with glue, leaving a raised line on the paper.
- Assist the child in tracing, as needed.
- Allow time to let the glue to dry thoroughly.
- Encourage the child to use his index finger to trace the shapes or letters of his name.

Another Idea

- Use glue shapes or letters for crayon rubbings. Place white paper on top of glue shapes and invite the child to color over them with a crayon.

PRE-WRITING SKILLS
Incline Writing Boards

Objectives

The child will develop an effective grasp of writing utensil.
The child will participate in pre-writing activities.

Materials

three-ring binder (3" size)
non-skid plastic drawer liner
large paper clips
variety of writing utensils, such as large
    washable markers
plain paper

Procedure

- Cut a piece of non-skid drawer liner to the size of the three-ring binder (adult-only step).
- Place the three-ring binder on top of the drawer liner, with the wide ring side of the binder facing away from the child. Tilt the binder slightly to the left if the child is right-handed or tilt it slightly to the right if he is left-handed.
- Help the child clip paper to the incline board using a large paper clip on the side.
- Encourage the child to draw or write on this inclined surface.

Another Idea

- The child can use the incline board on a table or on the floor for drawing, painting, and other pre-writing experiences.

PRE-WRITING SKILLS
Journal Drawing

Objectives
The child will have the opportunity to express himself on paper.

The child will participate in pre-writing activity.

The child will gain control of a writing tool.

Materials
unlined paper

variety of drawing tools, such as adult-size pencils, washable markers, or
crayons

Procedure
- Introduce the idea of journaling to the child. Explain that journaling is a way
  to tell a story.
- Encourage the child to participate in "journal drawing" by asking him to draw
  about a particular subject or theme. For example, while discussing places
  where people live, ask the child to draw a picture of his home.
- Ask the child to describe his "journal drawing" to you. Transcribe the child's
  words onto the paper and read the dictation back to the child.

More Ideas
- Some four-year-olds can write their names or write some letters. If he is able,
  encourage the child to sign his name and "write" about his drawing.
- Using journals throughout the year can be a great way to document a child's
  developmental progression of drawing and pre-writing skills.

PRE-WRITING SKILLS
Mirror, Mirror, on the Wall

Objectives

The child will draw or write on a vertical surface.

The child will participate in pre-writing activities.

Materials

wall mirror or large, stable mirror

dry-erase markers

eraser or dry cloth

Procedure

- Ask the child to stand facing the mirror.
- Encourage the child to use dry-erase markers to decorate himself on the mirror.
- Ideas include: adding hair, a mustache, a beard, a hair bow, earrings, clothes, glasses, a hat, and so on.
- When the child finishes his drawing, show him how to use the eraser to clean off the mirror.

More Ideas

- If the mirror is big enough, help the child trace around his entire body using a dry-erase marker.
- Encourage the child to walk away and look at his body shape.

PRE-WRITING SKILLS
Ribbon Drawing

Objectives
The child will develop shoulder strength needed for fine motor skills.
The child will form shapes, in preparation for writing and drawing.

Materials
ribbon 1"–2" wide

small wooden dowel rods ½"–1" in diameter and 8" –12" long

staple gun or duct tape

Procedure
- Cut the ribbon into 4' to 5' pieces. Staple or securely tape one end of the ribbon to the end of the dowel rod (adult-only step).
- In a place where there is adequate floor space, show the child how to hold the dowel and make the ribbon move through the air.
- Challenge the child to use his ribbon to draw shapes in the air, by asking, "Can you draw a circle?"
- Make a shape in the air using your ribbon, and see if the child can guess what shape it is. Then, ask the child to copy the shape you made using his own ribbon.

More Ideas
- Play music or sing songs about shapes and let the child make the shapes to the music.
- See if the child can write the letters of his name with the ribbons or imitate making simple letters, such as "O," "I," "T," and "L."

Shape Person

Objectives

The child will trace shapes.

The child will participate in pre-writing activity.

Materials

variety of shape stencils

washable markers

paper

Procedure

- Demonstrate one way to use shape stencils to draw a person. For example, show the child how to use a square for the head, a circle for the tummy, and triangles for legs and arms.

- Encourage the child to explore different ways to make a "shape person." He may trace the stencil or color inside the stencil.

- Ask the child to describe his person. Transcribe the child's description of his person onto the paper. Ask the child questions about his person, such as "What shapes did you use?"

Another Idea

- Provide glitter glue, jewels, and scrap pieces of material for the child to decorate his "shape person."

PRE-WRITING SKILLS
Sidewalk Shadows

Objectives
The children will develop drawing and tracing skills.

Materials
sidewalk chalk

Procedure
Note: This activity requires children to work together in pairs.

- Find a safe sidewalk or paved area.
- Explain that one child in the pair should lie down on the sidewalk. Remind this child to "act like a statue" and remain still.
- The other child should use sidewalk chalk to trace his partner's body, and make a "sidewalk shadow."
- Invite the children to change places so the statue child can trace his partner's outline on the ground.
- Encourage the children to add details to their "sidewalk shadows."

More Ideas
- Encourage the children to use chalk to write their names on their shadows.
- Bring buckets of water and paintbrushes out to the sidewalk. The children can make their shadows disappear by painting them with water.

Great for Groups

Simon Says

Objectives
The children will learn directional terms needed for writing.
The children will improve coordination.

Materials
none

Procedure
- Teach children the rules of "Simon Says."
- Play the part of Simon and give commands that include directional terms including up, down, under, and on top. For example:
  - Simon says, "Put your hands UP in the air."
  - Simon says, "Put your feet UNDER your chair."
  - Simon says, "Put your chin ON TOP OF your hand."

Another Idea
- Consider adding "left" and "right" terms to the game. Most four-year-olds have trouble differentiating between "left" and "right," so you should model the commands to help the children be successful. "Mirror" the motion (move the opposite side of your body, as though you were the children's reflection in a mirror) or stand with your back to the children and make the motions as you describe them. Both of these methods help the children imitate you as they follow the directions.

STRINGING/LACING
Bead Jewelry

Objectives
The child will gain experience stringing items.

The child will use two hands to create.

The child will improve **eye-hand coordination.**

Materials
variety of small beads (½" diameter or smaller)

plastic thread

non-skid plastic drawer liner cut into place mat-sized rectangles

child-safe scissors

Procedure
- Place beads on the non-skid mat so that the beads will not roll away.
- Ask the child to decide whether she wants to make a bracelet or a necklace.
- Provide child-safe scissors so the child can cut the thread to right length. Help the child cut the thread, if necessary.
- Tie a knot in the end of the thread.
- Encourage the child to string her beads to create jewelry.
- Help the child tie the two ends of the thread together when she finishes stringing the beads.

More Ideas
- Challenge the child to make a repeating pattern with the beads.
- Place the beads on the non-skid mat and help the child plan a pattern before stringing them. Talk with the child about the patterns.

Make Your Own Lacing Cards

Objectives

The child will gain experience with lacing.

The child will develop confidence in the use of tools.

Materials

old greeting cards

child-safe scissors

1-hole punch

yarn or string

duct tape

Procedure

- Set out the child-safe scissors and old greeting cards and invite the child to choose one of the cards. Show him how to cut the card along the fold, so that he ends up with two pieces that are the same size.
- Show the child how to use a 1-hole punch, and ask him to punch holes around the edges of the cards.
- Cut the yarn and cover one end with a piece of duct tape to make a tip. The child may need help with all parts of this step.
- Encourage the child to lace the yarn through his card.

More Ideas

- Use a long lace to string several cards together to form a line, and then hang up the string of cards as a decoration.

STRINGING / LACING

Tambourine

Objectives

The child will use various tools to create objects.

The child will gain confidence in tool use.

The child will develop lacing skills.

Materials

paper plates

buttons

stapler, 1-hole punch, and spoon

yarn and large markers or crayons

Procedure

- Invite the child to decorate the bottoms of two paper plates.
- Help the child staple the decorated paper plates together, keeping the staples around the outside, while leaving approximately 1" along the edge for hole-punching. Leave a 2" opening at the top of the plates for filling.
- Help the child use a spoon to put buttons inside joined plates, and assist him in stapling closed the remaining opening at the top.
- Encourage the child to use the 1-hole punch around the outside edge of plate construction.
- Give the child a length of yarn with a large knot at one end, to lace up the tambourine.
- Tie off the end of the yarn and trim the excess when finished (adult-only step).
- Turn on music or sing and invite the child to shake his tambourine to the beat.

Another Idea

- Use long ribbons instead of yard for lacing and leave the ends loose to use as streamers.

TOOL USE

Hair Salon and Barber Shop

Objectives

The child will improve bilateral hand skills.

The child will use fine motor skills in play.

The child will experiment with new tools.

Materials

large male and female dolls with hair

hairbrushes, combs, and curlers

foam soap and craft sticks for shaving

various decorative hair items such as clips, barrettes, rubber bands, and hair bows

cotton balls, cotton swabs, and makeup brushes or small paintbrushes

Procedure

- Talk to the child about what types of things happen in a hair salon and barber shop.
- Set out the various materials and encourage the child to use them to style his doll's hair.
- Observe the ways the child uses the different tools.
- Help the child learn the correct ways to use the grooming tools.

More Ideas

- Add play money to the area so the dolls can pay for his services. He can manipulate, count, and sort the coins and paper money.

TOOL USE
Kite Flying

Objectives

The child will use tools to create art.

The child will develop eye-hand coordination.

The child will express himself through construction of objects.

Materials

thick paper, such as oak tag, card stock, or construction paper

yarn or string

stapler, 1-hole punch, and tape

Procedure

- Show the child what a large diamond shape looks like.
- Then, ask him to draw two large diamond shapes (as close to the same size as he can) on his paper to cut out. **Note:** Many four-year-olds will draw a square or shape other than a diamond, which will work fine for this project.
- Show the child how to put the matching "diamonds" together using a stapler or tape.
- Help him cut a piece of yarn or string for the kite tail and punch a hole at the bottom of the kite.
- Invite the child to thread the yarn through the hole and help him tie a knot to secure it.
- Next, help him cut another piece of string to fly the kite with. Punch a hole at the top of the kite, thread the yarn through the hole, and tie a knot.
- Encourage him to hold onto the kite string and run around to "fly" his kite inside or outside.

Another Idea

- Set out markers and other materials and invite the child to decorate his kite.

TOOL USE

Making a Collage

Objectives

The child will gain experience using tools.

The child will participate in a pre-scissor activity.

Materials

variety of materials to cut or tear, including construction paper, greeting cards, junk mail, foil, tissue paper, wrapping paper, and newspaper

poster board or oak tag cut in half- or quarter-pieces

glue sticks and school glue

child-safe scissors

Procedure

- Talk with the child about methods for making a collage.
- Set out the various materials and talk about them with the child.
- Encourage him to choose, cut, and tear materials, and then glue these materials to the poster board or oak tag, making collages.
- Find a prominent place to display the collages he makes.

Another Idea

- Provide collage items that do not need to be cut, such as cotton balls, small pom-poms, felt scraps, pieces of yarn, and ribbon.

TOOL USE
Polka-Dot Shapes

Objectives
The child will use a 1-hole punch.
The child will create interesting designs.

Materials
construction paper cut in half, 5" x 7" index cards, or 5" x 7" cardstock
marker
1-hole punch

Procedure
- Using a marker, draw a shape (at least 4" across) on piece of paper. Make sure the lines of the shape are close to the edges of the paper.
- Show the child a 1-hole punch and invite him to practice using it. Demonstrate how to use the punch, if necessary.
- Encourage the child to punch holes along the edge of the shape. Help, as needed.

More Ideas
- Use the 1-hole punch to create simple lines or letters.
- Use the "polka-dot shape" as a template. Show the child how to place the "polka-dot shape" on another piece of paper and use markers to color in each hole. Lift the template to see the shape. Connect the dots to form the shape.

Chapter 5

Fine Motor Activities for Five-Year-Olds

What Can Most Five-Year-Old Children Do With Their Hands?

Five-year-olds are becoming more confident in their use of tools and materials like scissors, tape, glue, and 1-hole punches. Before they turn six, many children have established a consistent grasp pattern that they use for holding writing utensils and for self-care tasks. During the year, some five-year-olds will develop a growing interest in writing as a form of self-expression. Most five-year-olds learn to write their names and other letters of the alphabet that are interesting to them, such as letters for the words "mom" and "dad."

Typical fine motor development covers a broad range of skills and abilities, and each child will develop at her own pace. This list includes some of the fine motor skills that many five-year-old children develop over the course of the year. Remember, these skills are not presented in a specific developmental sequence, and serve only as a guideline for observing and teaching young children.

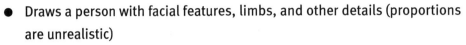

- Draws a person with facial features, limbs, and other details (proportions are unrealistic)
- Builds steps with small blocks
- Imitates drawing a diamond shape
- Writes first name and a few letters (may include letter omissions and/or letter reversals—letters may not be in a straight line)
- Creates symbolic representations of objects with clay or playdough (may not resemble the real objects)
- Creates symbolic representations of objects through drawing or painting (may not resemble the real objects)
- Signs and labels drawings (may include inventive spelling, letter omissions, and/or letter reversals)
- Laces shoes
- Uses a knife to spread/apply butter, jelly, and so on
- Puts together puzzles of at least six pieces
- Uses scissors to cut out small shapes and various designs (approximately 1" across)
- Uses scissors to cut non-paper materials such as yarn or tape
- Uses tools such as glue stick, 1-hole punch, stapler, and tape, with little supervision
- Uses fingers to act out fingerplays that require isolated finger movements, as in "Where Is Thumbkin?"
- Uses **dynamic tripod grasp** (holds tool with tips of thumb, index, and middle fingers; ring and pinky fingers bent) or **quadripod grasp** (holds tool with tips of thumb, index, middle, and ring fingers, with pinky bent) when using writing utensils

The activities in this chapter will help most five-year-old children expand their fine motor skills. Each activity focuses on at least one aspect of fine motor development, such as scissor use, pre-writing, **grasp, eye-hand coordination, in-hand manipulation,** or tool use. Many of the activities address a variety of fine motor skills that will benefit five-year-olds as they experiment with creative expression. All the activities are easy to incorporate into the classroom. Each will help teachers scaffold the five-year-old child's fine motor skills in a developmentally appropriate manner.

BILATERAL HAND SKILLS
Geoboards

Terms in bold are defined in the glossary, which begins on page 135

Objectives

The child will perform fine motor tasks that require finger strength.

The child will use two hands together (**bilateral coordination**) for fine motor tasks.

The child will begin developing **in-hand manipulation** skills.

Materials

Geoboard (can be commercially purchased or handmade (see More Ideas below))

rubber bands with good elasticity in a variety of sizes

Procedure

- Invite the child to explore the Geoboard and rubber bands.
- Demonstrate method of stretching a rubber band from one peg to the next. Form lines, shapes, or letters with the rubber bands.
- Encourage the child to make her own lines, shapes, or letters on the Geoboard with rubber bands.

More Ideas

- Make your own Geoboard. To make a Geoboard, you will need the following:
  square piece of wood (approximately 5" x 5")
  sandpaper
  25 finishing nails
  ruler
  hammer

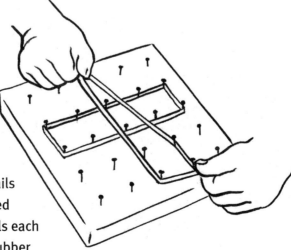

To make your own Geoboard, go to a building supply store and ask someone to cut a square piece of wood. Sand the edges until smooth. Use a hammer to insert 25 finishing nails into the wood in an evenly spaced pattern of five rows with five nails each 1" apart. To allow room for the rubber bands, nails should extend ½" out from the surface of the wood.

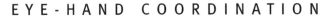

EYE-HAND COORDINATION
Graph Paper Art

Objectives

The child will refine the hand movements necessary for writing.

The child will develop good **eye-hand coordination**.

The child will use an age-appropriate grasp of writing utensil.

Materials

large grid (at least ¼") graph paper (may be printed for free off the Internet)

colored pencils

Procedure

● Give the child a piece of graph paper and colored pencils.

● Ask the child to color in the squares to create "Graph Paper Art."

● Encourage the child to color within the lines of the squares.

More Ideas

● Form letters by coloring in squares of the graph paper. Draw a letter on the graph paper for the child and then see if she can copy it.

● Give her graph paper and watercolors or tempera paint and small paintbrushes and encourage her to explore painting squares or other shapes and designs.

EYE-HAND COORDINATION
Making Tracks

Objectives
The child will develop small muscle control.

The child will write name and/or draw shapes.

The child will establish **eye-hand coordination.**

Materials
large sheets of paper and paper plates

various small toy vehicles, such as cars, trucks, vans, or construction vehicles

fingerpaint or tempera paint and markers

Procedure
- Write the child's name on a large sheet of paper. Use bubble-type letters that are large enough to serve as a track for small vehicles.
- Pour paint onto paper plates. Place some vehicles on the table so that the child can select them easily.
- Encourage the child to experiment with making tracks by rolling a vehicle through the paint and then rolling the vehicle over paper.
- Show the child her "Name Track." Encourage the child to roll a vehicle through the paint and trace the letters of her name with the vehicle to "make tracks."
- When the child begins to lose interest in the activity, give her a bowl of water and small sponges or brushes to wash off the vehicles. Set them on a paper towel to dry.

More Ideas
- Some children may be able to make their name tracks independently, without having to follow the letter outlines.
- Provide blank sheets of paper and encourage the child to make new letter tracks on her paper.

EYE-HAND COORDINATION

Stick Letters

Objectives
The child will use **eye-hand coordination** to perform fine motor tasks.

The child will form letters of the alphabet.

The child will participate in pre-writing activities.

Materials
craft sticks

scissors (adult-use only)

glue (squeezable or stick)

construction paper

washable markers

Procedure
- Cut several craft sticks crosswise into halves and fourths (adult-only step). After cutting them, sand the rough edges.
- Write capital letters on paper so that the child has an example to copy.
- Give the child various sizes of craft sticks.
- Ask the child to make "stick letters" by arranging the pieces of stick on the construction paper.

  Note: Letters with curves will be more challenging to make, but the child may use small pieces of craft sticks to form them.
- Invite the child to glue her letters to the construction paper, and then give them time to dry.
- Once the glue is dry, the child can use markers to trace around her "stick letters" on the paper or decorate the letters.

More Ideas
- Use sticks to write names or words that are of interest to the child.
- Some children may need you to write the letters on their paper, so they can place the craft sticks directly on the lines.

E Y E - H A N D   C O O R D I N A T I O N
Paper Flowers

Objectives
The child will use scissors to cut thin paper.

The child will fold paper.

The child will develop **eye-hand coordination** for use in play.

Materials
thin, 8 ½" X 11" copying paper in various colors

child-safe scissors (sharp enough to cut thin paper)

chenille sticks

Procedure
- After the child selects the paper for her flowers, help her use the scissors to cut paper in half to form a 8 ½ x 5 ½ rectangle.

- Demonstrate how to accordion-pleat the paper, starting on the long side of the paper. Help the child as needed.
- Ask the child to hold the pleated paper, while you help her wind one end of a chenille stick around the center of the paper.
- Encourage the child to separate layers of the paper by gently pulling the paper apart at the edges of the flower.

Another Idea
- Place the flowers into a piece of Styrofoam and then inside the "Painted Flower Pot" (see "Painted Flower Pots" page 128) for a child-made gift or decoration.

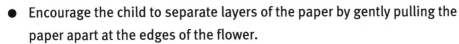

FINGER ISOLATION
Where Is Thumbkin?

Objectives

The child will coordinate eyes and hands for fingerplay.

The child will be able to move individual fingers (**finger isolation**).

Materials

Procedure

- Sing the song, "Where Is Thumbkin?" and demonstrate the related hand movements as you go.
- Show the child how to hold her fingers down with her thumb to help isolate one finger for movement.

  Note: The middle and ring fingers are typically the hardest to isolate and individualize. The child may need to hold down the other fingers until she masters this new motor pattern.

More Ideas

- "This Old Man" is another good fingerplay that gives the child the opportunity to develop her isolated finger-movement skills.
- Fingerplays that involve counting on the fingers will help the child develop her isolated finger-movement skills.

G R A S P

Clay Writing Board

Objectives

The child will establish an effective grasp of writing tools.

The child will build finger strength.

Materials

small cookie sheet or pizza pan (pan with small edge)

modeling clay (single color works best)

stylus (a wooden or metal tool used to make indentations in clay available for purchase at a craft store.) You can make your own stylus by using a pen with the ink barrel removed, or a chopstick.

resealable plastic bag large enough to hold a cookie sheet or pizza pan

Procedure

- Invite the child to help you flatten modeling clay evenly over the cookie sheet, so that the clay is ¼" or ½" thick.
- Show the child the stylus and explain that it is a tool that artists sometimes use to make marks in clay. Invite the child to experiment with making different kinds of marks with the stylus on the clay.
- Demonstrate how to use the stylus to write letters or draw shapes on the "Clay Writing Board." Show how to use your fingers to erase the letters in the clay by tracing them with your index finger and pressing the clay into its original flat shape.
- Encourage the child to write her name, letters, or shapes in the clay. If necessary, help the child by writing the letters first and then letting her trace over them with the stylus.
- When not in use, store the clay for the "Clay Writing Board" in a resealable plastic bag.

More Ideas

- Give the child letter or shape templates that she may trace in the clay.
- Place the "Clay Writing Board" in the Home Living, Cooking, or Restaurant Center. Children can draw pizzas, cookies, and other items on the board.

105

GRASP
Cotton Swab Painting

Objectives

The child will develop an effective grasp for use with writing utensils.
The child will use new tools to create artwork.

Materials

cotton swabs, one for each color
tempera paint, various colors
shallow containers for paint
paper (no larger than 8 ½" x 11")
easel or wall for attaching paper

Procedure

● Place paper for painting on an easel or taped to a wall.
● Encourage the child to use cotton swabs as her paintbrushes to create art.
  She can use the tips of cotton swabs to dab paint on paper and create
  polka dots.

Another Idea

● Give the child a very small piece of paper to create mini artwork using the
  cotton swabs. A 3" x 5" index card works well.

GRASP
"Itsy Bitsy" Writing Utensils

Objectives

The child will establish an appropriate grasp of writing tools.

The child will use various tools for writing or drawing.

Materials

paper

golf pencils or small pencils that are less than 3" in length

pieces of crayons less than 3" in length

storage containers for pencils and crayons

Procedure

- Label storage containers for golf pencils and small pieces of crayons as "Itsy Bitsy."
- Provide "Itsy Bitsy" pencils and crayons for writing and drawing.
- Encourage the child to use the "Itsy Bitsy" writing utensils.

More Ideas

- Provide small pieces of chalk for the child to practice writing and drawing on sidewalk or chalk board.
- Read a book or tell a story about a small person or animal who was "Itsy Bitsy." One favorite is "The Itsy Bitsy Spider."

GRASP
Water Droppers

Objectives
The child will develop effective grasp for tools and utensils.
The child will build strength in fingers.

Materials
pennies and quarters
eyedropper or **pipette**
containers of water for filling eyedropper
newspaper or plastic to protect table from
   water spills

Procedure
- Show the child how to fill up an
  eyedropper with water. Show her how
  to squeeze the eyedropper gently to
  make single drops of water.
- Give the child a penny and a quarter.
  Ask her to guess how many drops of
  water each coin will hold.
- Invite the child to drip water slowly onto the face of each coin to see how
  many water drops each coin can hold. Help her count, if necessary.
- Compare results by asking questions, such as, "How many water drops did
  the penny hold?" "How much did the quarter hold?" "Which coin held more
  water drops?" "Why?"

Another Idea
- Add a few drops of dishwashing liquid to the water container. Repeat the
  experiment. The dishwashing liquid reduces the surface tension of the water
  so the coins will not hold the water drops.

IN-HAND MANIPULATION
Coin Match

Objectives

The child will perform fine motor activities that require eye-hand coordination.
The child will develop in-hand manipulation skills necessary for fine motor
  tasks.

Materials

variety of coins, including pennies, nickels, and quarters

small bowls or plastic containers for coins

paper

black pen or marker

Procedure

- Trace around different-sized coins to make patterns. Keep the pattern very simple, such as quarter, penny, quarter, penny; or nickel, nickel, penny, nickel, nickel, penny. Trace no more than 10 coins on each piece of paper.
- Invite the child to sort pennies, nickels, and quarters, and place them in separate containers.
- Give her a coin pattern to replicate.
- Encourage her to select coins from the pre-sorted bowls and match them to their corresponding spots by size.
- When she finishes, place one coin into each container, and then ask her to sort the coins back into the proper containers.

Another Idea

- Create more patterns by tracing around different coins on paper, or you can make coin rubbings rather than tracing around the circumference of the coins.

IN-HAND MANIPULATION
Piggy Banks

Objectives

The child will manipulate small objects in her hand.

The child will insert small objects into a small opening.

The child will use a pincer grasp to place small objects.

Materials

various sizes of clear, plastic jars with lids

foam coin holders (used by collectors to display coins), foam ring holders (used
    by jewelers to showcase rings), or square pieces of foam at least 1" thick

sharp knife or X-ACTO™ knife (adult-use only)

variety of coins, including pennies, nickels, dimes, and quarters

Preparation (adult only)

- To make a piggy bank, wash and remove the label from the plastic jar so that
  it is completely transparent. Cut a slit in the top of the jar lid. The slit must be
  large enough to place a quarter through it.

- To make a coin holder, cut a slit in the top of the foam. The slit must be wide
  enough and deep enough to hold quarters. Coins should sit slightly above
  the foam so that your child can remove them with his fingertips.

Procedure

- Place a variety of coins flat on a table or other hard surface.
- Encourage the child to fill up the piggy bank or coin holder with coins.

More Ideas

- Make this a game and see how many coins the child can put in the piggy
  bank or coin holder in one minute. Help the child count the coins while
  putting them inside or when she finishes.

- Label jars with a picture of a particular coin, or place one coin into the jar
  to get the child started. Challenge the child to sort the coins into the
  specified jars.

PRE-WRITING SKILLS

Furry Letters

Objectives

The child will use **in-hand manipulation** skills in play.

The child will recognize letters of the alphabet.

The child will form letters of the alphabet.

Materials

chenille sticks

3" x 5" or 5" x 7" index cards, heavy paper, or card stock

marker

scissors (adult-use only)

Procedure

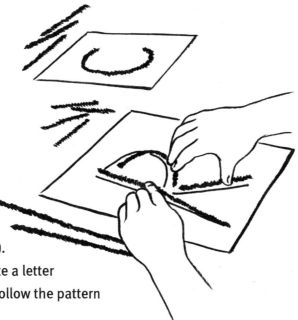

- On each card, write a letter large enough to use as a pattern for chenille sticks (adult only).

- Cut several of the chenille sticks in half; also cut some into fourths (adult only). Make three sizes of chenille sticks (whole, ½, ¼).

- Show the child how to create a letter by bending the chenille to follow the pattern on the cards.

- Encourage her to make "Furry Letters" that spell her name or other words of interest.

More Ideas

- The child may glue the "Furry Letter Names/Words" onto heavy paper.

- Play a game with the "Furry Letters." Place the letters in a shoebox or storage container. The child closes her eyes, reaches into the box, and pulls out a letter. See if the child can identify the letter by touch.

PRE-WRITING SKILLS

PRE-WRITING SKILLS
Glitter Letters

Objectives

The child will gain experience with letters.

The child will manipulate a variety of materials.

The child will develop **eye-hand coordination**.

Materials

construction paper, marker, and glue

small bowls or containers

cotton swabs or craft sticks

glitter (store in jars for shaking or in open containers to sprinkle with fingers)

Note: For easy clean-up, cover the work surface with a shower curtain, newspaper, or vinyl tablecloth.

Procedure

- Use a marker to write letters or the child's name on construction paper.
- Put glue in one container and glitter in another one, if you are not using jars.
- Ask the child to use a cotton swab or craft stick to trace each letter with glue.
- Encourage the child either to shake glitter from a jar or to use her fingers to sprinkle glitter over each letter.
- Gently shake the completed paper to remove excess glitter, and allow the paper to dry.

More Ideas

- Once the glitter letters are dry, the child can use her fingers to trace over the letters. Ask her, "How do the letters feel?"

PRE-WRITING SKILLS
Rainbow Letters

Objectives

The child will write letters.

The child will hold paper in place while writing.

The child will use various utensils for writing.

Materials

plain white paper

colored pencils or thin washable markers

Procedure

- Write some letters or the child's name on white paper. Space the letters out so the child has plenty of room to trace around them.
- Demonstrate how to trace around the outside of a letter, using a different color each time. When you finish, you will have a "rainbow" letter.
- Give the child her papers and encourage her to trace around the letters to make her own "rainbow" letters or words.

More Ideas

- Provide glitter pens or watercolor paints and small brushes so the child can make "rainbow" letters with different materials.
- Provide child-safe scissors so the child may cut out her "rainbow" letters.

PRE-WRITING SKILLS
Sandbox Writing

Objectives

The child will participate in a multi-sensory activity that will facilitate writing.

The child will develop finger strength.

The child will gain confidence in writing ability.

Materials

shoeboxes and solid-color contact paper (red, blue, black, and green work well)

white sand (clean and sterilized, available at home improvement stores)

letters of the alphabet for children to model

Procedure

- Cover the inside bottom of a shoebox with contact paper and coat the bottom of the box with white sand until the sand is ½" deep (adult-only step).
- Provide examples of letters to model, and encourage the child to write letters in the "sandbox" using her index finger. If she presses her finger hard enough, she will be able to see the colored contact paper under the sand.
- Invite the child to shake the sandbox gently from side to side or smooth the sand with her hand to erase her letters.

More Ideas

- Add several drops of water to the sand or mist the sand with a spray bottle to moisten it. The slight increase in resistance in the sand will build more finger strength, as the child continues to form letters with her fingers.
- Provide tools such as a craft stick, drinking straw, or chopstick with which the child may practice writing in the sand.

PRE-WRITING SKILLS
Sandpaper Writing

Objectives
The child will expand repertoire of writing skills.

The child will participate in tactile pre-writing experiences.

The child will develop grasp strength.

Materials
sandpaper of various grits (coarse, medium, or fine grit will work)

plain paper (copy or drawing)

writing tools, such as golf pencils, crayons, or thin markers

letters or words for children to copy

Procedure
- Place the plain paper on top of the sandpaper.
- Ask the child which letters or words she wants to copy.
- As she writes on the paper, the sandpaper will add extra resistance to the writing and texture to the writing experience.
- If you use different grits of sandpaper, talk about how they feel different and how the writing looks different.

Another Idea
- Set out chalk for your child to write with directly on the sandpaper. Then encourage your child to use her fingers to try to erase the letters.

Write a Little Note

Objectives

The child will write letters, or symbols that look like letters.

The child will use a developmentally appropriate grasp of the writing utensil.

The child will use small movements of the fingers for writing.

Materials

small sticky notes (from 1"–3" square)

golf pencils or short adult pencils (less than 3" long)

Procedure

- Give the child several sticky notes and a small pencil.
- Talk about the different "notes" that people write throughout the day, such as phone messages, "to-do" lists, wish lists, or notes to our friends.
- Encourage the child to write a little note and read it to a friend or an adult.

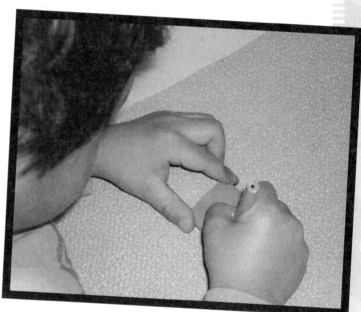

More Ideas

- Stick the child's "little note" on a larger sheet of paper and, as a method of documentation, ask the child to tell you what she wrote on her note, and transcribe the text onto the larger paper.
- Place sticky notes or small notepads and small pencils in the Home Living or Restaurant Center. These are good for making grocery lists or for taking food orders from customers.

PUZZLES

Make Your Own Puzzle

Objectives

The child will put together puzzles.

The child will create art using markers.

The child will create art using scissors.

Materials

thick paper, such as oak tag, card stock, or poster board

thin and thick markers

child-safe scissors

resealable plastic bags

Procedure

- Give the child a piece of thick paper, no larger than 8 ½" x 11". If using poster board, turn paper to the non-glossy side.
- Explain the methods for making a puzzle including:
  - Use markers to draw a picture or design that will fill up the entire piece of paper.
  - Cut the picture into 8–12 puzzle pieces.
  - Put the puzzle together.
- Assist the child by making sure she uses ample color in her pictures and designs. This will make the puzzle easier to put together.
- Help the child cut the paper into puzzle pieces, ensuring that the pieces are not too small to manipulate.
- Encourage the child to practice putting her puzzle together.
- Place the child's puzzle into a resealable plastic bag and label with her name and a short description of the puzzle (for example, "my house" or "rainbow").

More Ideas

- Add small rulers and/or templates to the materials. The children can use them to draw lines or make designs for their puzzles.
- Place a few puzzles in the Library Center or Fine Motor Center so that children can practice putting together various puzzles.

SCISSOR SKILLS
Animal Masks

Objectives

The child will use scissors to create artwork.

The child will gain experience with drawing utensils.

Materials

thick white paper such as construction paper, card stock, or oak tag (8 ½" x 11")

variety of drawing utensils such as color pencils, thin markers, small crayons, glitter pens, or paint pens

child-safe scissors, 1-hole punch, and yarn or string

Procedure

- Cut out several masks using this illustration as a guide (adult-only step).
- Ask the child to use a pencil, marker, crayon, or pen to trace around the mask on the thick paper.
- Provide various drawing materials for the child to use to decorate the mask and create an animal face.
- Help the child cut out her mask, if necessary. Be sure the eye holes are well-positioned so the child can see.
- Guide the child as she uses the 1-hole punch to place one hole on either side of the mask.
- Tie yarn or string through the holes to fit the mask to the child's face.

More Ideas

- Ask the child questions about the animal she has "become," such as, "What sound do you make?" or "How do you walk?"
- Act out a simple story using the mask, and make additional masks for other characters in the story.

SCISSOR SKILLS
Paper Dolls

Objectives

The child will create art with scissors.

The child will develop **eye-hand coordination**.

The child will develop **bilateral hand skills**.

Materials

thick paper such as cardstock or oaktag

scissors (adult-use only)

child-safe scissors

variety of paper, including paper with designs, such as scrapbook paper, greeting cards, construction paper, foil, and sandpaper

various scrap materials for decorating a doll, including yarn, beads, buttons, cotton fabric, and sequins

glue

small pieces of chalk, crayons, markers, or stubby pencils

resealable plastic storage bags

Procedure

- Cut out paper dolls using the pattern on page 120 as a guide (adult-only step). The dolls should be 6"–8" tall.
- Give the child a variety of materials and glue to decorate the dolls.
- Suggest that she add faces and hair to her dolls using glue, yarn, beads, buttons, crayons, and markers. Allow the dolls to dry.
- Remove the glue from the work area, and give her various pieces of paper and cotton fabric.
- Talk about how to make clothes for her dolls. She can make several different clothing items to dress her dolls.
- Encourage the child to use the chalk, crayons, markers, or pencils to draw patterns for the doll's clothing. Demonstrate how to trace around the dolls on the paper or fabric.
- Provide the child-safe scissors so she can cut out the clothing and use it to dress her dolls by placing the dolls flat on the tabletop and covering them with the clothing cutouts. It's best not to glue the clothing to the dolls so that she can change their outfits.

More Ideas

- Store the paper dolls and clothing in labeled, resealable plastic bags, so the child can revisit this activity to make more clothes for her dolls.
- Read the child's favorite fairy tale and then make "costumes" to dress the characters from the story. For instance, the child can make a red cape for Little Red Riding Hood or a pirate costume for Captain Hook.

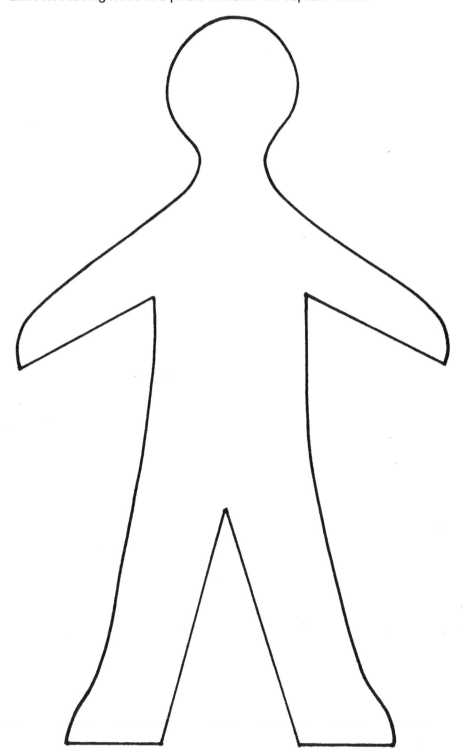

SCISSOR SKILLS
Paper Mobile

Objectives
The child will use scissors to make artwork.

The child will develop **eye-hand coordination**.

Materials
thin paper (cut in squares) in solid colors, such as copy paper, tracing paper, or
    wrapping paper

pencils and child-safe scissors

Procedure
● Cut paper into 6" x 6" or 8" x 8" squares (adult-only step).
● Model for the child how to fold her piece of paper (assist the child if necessary):
  ◦ Fold the paper in half, with opposite corners touching, to form a triangle.
  ◦ Fold the paper in half again, to form a smaller triangle.
● Draw alternating lines, about ½" apart on paper triangle, as shown in the illustration (adult-only step).
● Encourage the child to cut directly on the lines, making sure not to cut all the way across the paper.
● Gently open the paper to form a "Paper Mobile."

More Ideas
● Staple a string to the top of the mobile to hang it.
● Staple two "Paper Mobiles" together at each corner and then gently pull apart to make accordion-like paper art.
● Provide markers, crayons, or glitter glue for the child to decorate her mobile after she cuts it out.

SCISSOR SKILLS
Snowflakes

Objectives

The child will use scissors in art creations.

The child will fold paper.

The child will coordinate the use of two hands in play.

Materials

white paper (cut into squares) that is good for folding, such as copy paper or
    drawing paper

child-safe scissors

Procedure

- Cut pieces of paper into 4" x 4" to 8" x 8" squares (adult-only step).
- Demonstrate the following method for folding paper and help the child, as needed. Draw lines on the paper to help the child know where to fold.
  - Fold the paper in half, with opposite corners touching, to form a triangle.
  - Fold the paper in half again, to form a smaller triangle.
- Show the child a method for snipping or cutting the edges of the paper triangle.
- Open the paper to reveal a snowflake.

More Ideas

- Use waxed paper or foil wrapping paper to make unusual snowflakes.
- provide glitter glue and sparkles with which the child may decorate her snowflakes.

STRINGING/LACING
Lace Up Those Shoes

Objectives

The child will gain experience with lacing and tying.

The child will participate in activities to improve **eye-hand coordination**.

The child will develop self-care skills.

Materials

variety of adult or large children's shoes that lace, such as tennis shoes, dress shoes, boots, or unusual shoes

various shoelaces with good tips, including leather, fabric, and elastic

Procedure

- Remove the laces from several pairs of shoes (adult-only step).
- Challenge the child to pair up the shoes.
- Demonstrate for the child a method for lacing shoes, using verbal directions, as you go, such as:
  - Start at the two bottom holes.
  - Pull the shoelace through until the two sides of the laces are equal.
  - String the lace through each hole.
- Encourage the child to hold a shoe in her lap or put the shoe on her foot.
- Invite the child to try to lace and tie the shoes.
- After the child finishes lacing her shoes, encourage her to put on a fashion show and walk around in her laced-up shoes.

More Ideas

- There are various ways to lace shoes. You can cross the laces or lace the shoes straight up the sides. Encourage the child to try her own lacing patterns.
- Place the shoes and laces in the Home Living Center or another Learning Center.
- Place the laces that correspond to each shoe in a small plastic bag labeled with a photograph of the matching shoe. This will help the child select laces that will work effectively for the shoes.

TOOL USE
Clay Sculptures: Self-Portrait

Objectives

The child will participate in activities to improve hand skills.

The child will experiment with a variety of tools in play.

The child will use hands to create original work.

Materials

modeling clay

wax paper

variety of tools, including rolling pins, stylus (piece of wood shaped like a
   pencil for carving clay), pens with ink barrel removed, craft sticks,
   toothpicks, child-safe scissors, plastic knives, and small mallets

unbreakable mirror(s) (hand-held or standing)

air-tight storage containers

Procedure

● Engage the child in a discussion about how artists make sculptures. Show
   the child pictures and read about sculptures. You will find interesting books
   in your local library. Ask the librarian to help you find books about sculptors
   both classic and contemporary. Good examples would be Michaelangelo,
   Rodin, Henry Moore, Alexander Calder, or Ruth Asawa. Talk about how artists
   create self-portraits.

● Place a piece of modeling clay on wax paper for the child, and show her the
   various tools she can use to create her sculpture.

● Encourage the child to make a self-portrait. Ask the child to sculpt her head
   or her head and body, depending on the amount of clay available.

● Suggest that the child examine herself in the mirror before and during the
   process.

● Allow the child ample time to explore the modeling clay and tools.

● Demonstrate a variety of techniques for using tools to mold, carve, or
   manipulate clay.

● This project may continue over several days. Store the clay in air-tight
   containers overnight, or cover the sculptures with moist towels so that the
   clay will not harden.

T O O L   U S E
Magic Rocket

Objectives

The child will develop confidence in using hands to construct objects.

The child will use tape in creative projects.

Materials

paper towel rolls

wrapping paper rolls

paper plates

child-safe scissors

tape (masking, duct, or electrical)

construction paper

various materials for decorating (markers,
    crayons, star stickers, or paint)

Procedure

- Set the various materials out on a work surface.
- Show the child a picture or read a book about a rocket or spaceship. Two good choices are *Roaring Rockets (Amazing Machines)* by Tony Mitton and Ant Parker and *On the Launch Pad: A Counting Book about Rockets* by Michael Dahl.
- Encourage the child to build her own "Magic Rocket" by taping materials together. Paper plates can be cut in half to make wings or a propeller. Use the construction paper to make a cone-shaped tip of the rocket ship.
- Assist the child by holding materials or cutting tape, as needed.
- Once she finishes constructing her "Magic Rocket," she can decorate it with markers, crayons, stickers, or paint.

More Ideas

- Create a telescope. Tape 2 or 3 paper towel rolls end to end to form a long telescope.
- Create binoculars. Cut a paper towel roll in half. Tape the two parts side to side to form binoculars. Your child can then decorate the telescope or binoculars and use his new tools to watch his rocket take off and sail into outer space.

TOOL USE
Nature Prints

Objectives

The child will use a variety of objects to create art.

The child will develop an effective grasp of tools.

Materials

collection of objects from outdoors (flat objects with texture work best) such as
leaves, bark, grass, flowers, rocks, or shells

thin, white paper such as typing, tracing, or onionskin paper

small crayons and pieces of crayons

Procedure

- Engage the children in a discussion about print making and how to make art with prints.
- Demonstrate one method of print making by placing a flat object under a piece of paper, and using a piece of crayon to rub across the paper.
- Discuss the collection of nature items.
- Encourage the child to explore the objects and make her own prints.

Another Idea

- Discuss with the child some of the reasons why certain objects do not make a print. Allow the child to collect items from around the room to discover if they will make a print.

TOOL USE
Off to Work I Go!

Objectives

The child will experiment with tools that develop small muscle dexterity.

The child will gain confidence in fine motor abilities.

The child will explore and engage in activities that facilitate **eye-hand coordination**.

Materials

briefcase or messenger bag

variety of paper used at work, such as address books, notepads, sticky notes, memo pads, receipt books, and order forms

variety of writing utensils, such as pencils, thin markers, washable pens, and yellow, green, or pink washable markers to use as highlighters

variety of tools, such as 1-hole punch, ruler, tape, and glue sticks

cell phone (play or non-functioning)

calculator

Procedure

● Organize the materials inside the briefcase.

● Talk with the child about the function of a briefcase and common tools that it may contain.

● Encourage the child to explore the briefcase and use the tools in play.

More Ideas

● Place the briefcase in the Home Living Center to stimulate more fine motor play.

● Put a wallet or coin purse with coins inside the briefcase to add more interest.

TOOL USE

Painted Flower Pots

Objectives

The child will manipulate tools in play.

The child will create art with a variety of materials.

The child will use an effective grasp of tools.

Materials

terra cotta flowerpots

acrylic paints

small paintbrushes

foam stamps

clear acrylic spray

vinyl tablecloth, shower curtain, or newspaper to
  keep work surface clean

paint shirts for children

Procedure

- Provide the child with a flowerpot. Set out the various decorative materials.

- Encourage the child to use paintbrushes and/or foam stamps to decorate her flowerpot.

- Spray the painted pot with clear acrylic spray (adult-only step) and allow it to dry.

More Ideas

- Suggest that the child sign her art by writing her name or initials on her flowerpot with a small paintbrush. Or, write her name on the bottom of the pot with a permanent marker.

- Fill the pot with a flower or plant or ask the child if she would like to make "Paper Flowers" to place inside (see page 103).

GRASP
Treasure Box

Objectives

The child will develop an effective grasp for use with writing utensils.

The child will use a variety of materials to create artwork.

Materials

jewelry boxes or small boxes with lids

various small items for decorating boxes such as sequins, tiny beads, and
　　buttons

small paintbrushes or cotton swabs

glue

coins, shells, or other "treasures"

Procedure

- Encourage the children to use paintbrushes or cotton swabs to paint the treasure boxes with glue.
- After the boxes are painted, the children can decorate them with small items.
- Separate the box lids and bottoms to let them dry separately.
- When the boxes and lids are dry, put each lid back on its box, and then provide several coins, shells, or other treasures, and invite the children to place them in the boxes.
- Invite one child to "bury the treasure" by hiding one treasure box somewhere in the room or nearby outside. Other children then become treasure hunters who try to find the buried treasure.

More Ideas

- Provide paper and markers or pencils for the children to draw treasure maps to help the treasure hunters find the hidden treasure.

Answers to Questions from Preschool Teachers

Should preschoolers use "fat" or "skinny" pencils?

Three-year-old children should typically use large writing and drawing utensils. Their small, weak fingers and less developed grasps will work best with bigger tools like large markers and paintbrushes. Provide four- and five-year-olds with a variety of smaller writing utensils such as normal-sized pencils, golf pencils, small crayons, thin markers, and small paintbrushes. These little tools will promote a better grasp and improved coordination.

What type of paper is best for cutting?

For preschoolers who are just learning to cut, thick paper works best. Suggestions include card stock, magazine inserts (cards), brown paper bags, index cards, and construction paper. Once a preschooler is able to cut stiff paper easily, the child may then progress to standard paper. Use thin paper, such as foil, wax paper, magazines, or newspaper with a child who is adept at using scissors and standard paper. Make sure the scissors are sharp and open and close smoothly so that the young child will be successful with cutting.

When should a child have an established "handedness?"

Most three- and four-year-olds will have an obvious hand preference. However, as children are developing their **bilateral (**both) hand skills during the fifth year of life, they may alternate use of hands. Most children have a well-established hand preference for fine motor activities by age six.

When should a child use an adult-like grasp of the pencil?

The majority of children between the ages of 4 ½ and 6 years will utilize a mature grasp of writing utensils. This adult-like grasp typically means that the child holds the pencil with the fingertips and has more control of the pencil. A child's acquisition of grasp will be affected by things such as experience, muscle tone, and cognitive abilities.

What is the best type of pencil grasp for a four-year-old child to use?

There are several grasps that are considered efficient for four- and five-year-olds. These grasps include two main components:

1. Fingertips on the end of the pencil.
2. An open web space between the thumb and fingers (thumb and fingers form a circular position, so that you can see the palm of the hand).

Many children prefer to use a **dynamic tripod grasp**, holding the writing utensil between the thumb, index, and middle fingers. A **quadripod grasp** that incorporates the thumb, index, middle, and ring fingers is another effective and commonly used grasp.

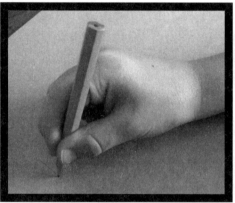

Dynamic Tripod Grasp   **Quadripod Grasp**

When should a child be able to tie her shoes?

Most children learn to tie their shoes some time during kindergarten. At this time, a child will usually have the bilateral hand skills, grasp, and eye-hand coordination necessary to complete this complex self-help skill. A child who primarily wears slip-on or Velcro-closure shoes will lack the experience with tying shoes and may develop this skill later.

When should a child be able to write her name?

Many five-year-olds are able to write their first names independently. Some five-year-olds will also be able to write a few letters that are not in their first names, but which the children find interesting (for example, "M," "O," "M").

What if a preschooler writes his name backwards?

It is typical for preschoolers to write letters backwards or to orient their names backwards across the page. Many children demonstrate letter reversals through the end of first grade. Four- and five-year-olds need opportunities to observe, imitate, and copy letters and words in a literacy-rich environment that includes books, signs, labels, and other reading materials.

If a preschooler holds her pencil in an awkward manner, should I try to change it?

It is important first to consider the child's age and developmental level. It would not be uncommon for a young, inexperienced preschooler to use what may look like an awkward grasp of a pencil. Young preschoolers may also grasp a pencil in a different way each time they hold one. Grasp is based on habit. So, whatever grasp the child consistently uses in later preschool and kindergarten will probably be the grasp she utilizes into adulthood. Make sure that the child participates in activities that promote the foundations of pre-writing (see Chapter 1) and that the child is using the appropriate size of pencil. If a four- or five-year-old child is consistently holding utensils with an awkward and inappropriate grasp, then consider demonstrating the proper way to grasp a writing tool and gently reposition the pencil in the child's hand. Also try introducing the child to a pencil grip (such as a triangle grip) to help the child learn to hold the pencil more appropriately.

What if a preschooler holds his scissors upside down?

It is typical for two- and three-year-olds to hold scissors upside down. Preschoolers often use this pattern if they have not had much experience with pre-scissor activities. Provide the child with pre-scissor activities, such as picking up objects with tongs, squeezing water out of turkey basters, or using a 1-hole punch on paper. Be sure to model the proper way to hold scissors and you may give "thumb on top" verbal reminders. With enough practice, the preschooler should develop into the next stage of scissor use—holding the scissors appropriately and snipping paper.

When is it appropriate to begin teaching young a child how to write the letters of the alphabet?

Children should be able to copy simple lines, shapes, and their first names before practicing the proper formation of uppercase and lowercase letters of the alphabet. Most children are not developmentally ready to begin handwriting instruction until the second half of kindergarten. Young children should NOT be sitting at tables and using handwriting workbook pages. Instead, provide children with a variety of materials that include the alphabet and words, so that they have something to copy, if they are interested.

What type of paper is appropriate to use in Pre-K writing activities?

It is recommended that preschoolers write on plain paper with no lines. Most four- and five-year-olds do not have the visual perceptual skills or the fine motor control necessary to write letters accurately on a line or between two lines.

Elementary paper that includes the dotted line in the middle of two solid lines is even more visually confusing than wide-ruled paper, and so it is best not to use it at all in preschool.

What if a preschooler is using fine motor skills that are well below age-appropriate level?

Begin by informing the child's parents or guardians of your concern. Then, contact your local school system's **Child Find Program** or Special Education Program to make a referral. The child should receive a thorough occupational therapy evaluation to assess her fine motor abilities. An occupational therapist who specializes in young children can make recommendations for the preschool classroom and provide fine motor intervention for the preschooler.

Glossary

Bilateral Hand Skills: The ability to use both hands together to accomplish a task.

Child Find Program: A publicly-funded program under the *Individuals with Disabilities Education Act (IDEA)* intended to identify, locate, and evaluate/assess infants and toddlers with potential developmental delays or disabilities.

Cognitive Development: The process of thinking, learning, perception, and reasoning.

Developmentally Appropriate: Activities and educational experiences that match the child's age and stage of development.

Digital Pronate Grasp: Object is held with all fingers, wrist straight, and forearm moves with hand. Typical grasp for 2- to 3-year-olds.

Dynamic Tripod Grasp: Object is held with fingertips of thumb, index, and middle fingers; ring and little fingers bent; hand moves separately from forearm. Typical grasp for 4½- to 6-year-olds. Mature grasp pattern.

Eye-Hand Coordination: The ability to use fine motor skills to accomplish a task that the eyes and brain want to complete.

Fine Motor: Movement of the small muscles in the fingers, hands, and forearms (for example, writing, cutting with scissors, stringing beads, or drawing). Another term for "small motor."

Finger Isolation: Using one finger (for example, pointing).

Grasp: Hold with fingers.

Gross Motor Skills: Movement of the large muscles in the arms, legs, and back (for example, walking, running, or kicking). Another term for "large motor."

Hand Dominance/Handedness: The hand that develops strength, skill, and precision to perform fine motor tasks. A preference for using one hand over the other.

In-Hand Manipulation: Adjustment of object in the hand, after grasp.

Occupational Therapist (OT): A healthcare professional who helps persons overcome physical or social problems due to illness or disability. OTs are skilled in adapting the environment so that a child can participate in the occupations of childhood: play, school, and self-care.

Open-Ended Activities: Materials or projects used to create without fixed limits or restrictions. For example, drawing on a blank sheet of paper rather than in a coloring book.

Pencil Grasp: How a person holds a writing tool.

Pencil Grip: Tool added to pencil to help correct an ineffective pencil grasp.

Pincer Grasp: Using index finger and thumb to hold an object.

Pipette: A syringe-like device used to pick up and dispense a liquid.

Proprioceptive Sense (Proprioception): The unconscious awareness of sensations coming from the muscles and joints that provides information about where each part of the body is and how it is moving.

Quadripod Grasp: Held with fingertips of thumb, index, middle, and ring fingers; little finger bent; hand moves separately from forearm. Mature grasp pattern.

Reciprocal Hand Skills: Using one hand to do one thing while the other hand does something different. For example, when cutting with scissors, one hand holds the paper and the other hand manipulates the scissors.

Release: Using fingers to let go of an object.

Static Tripod Grasp: Held with crude approximation of thumb, index, and middle fingers; ring and little fingers are only slightly bent; grasped high on the utensil. Typical grasp for 3½- to 4-year-olds.

Stylus: A pointed metal or wooden tool used to make indentations in the support surface.

Tactile Sense: The sensory system responsible for identifying touch input, understanding what has been felt, and preparing for a response.

References

Beery, K. E. 1997. *The developmental test of visual-motor integration* 5th ed. Austin, TX: Pro-Ed.

Benbow, M. 1990. *Loops and other groups, a kinesthetic writing system.* Tucson, AZ: Therapy Skill Builders.

Bredekamp, S., & C. Copple, eds. 1997. *Developmentally appropriate practices in early childhood programs.* Washington, DC: National Association for the Education of Young Children. **Author note**: Although this is an older reference, it offers a great deal of information on fine motor development.

Bredekamp, S., & C. Copple, eds. 2009. *Developmentally appropriate practices in early childhood programs.* Washington, DC: National Association for the Education of Young Children.

Case-Smith, J., & C. Pehoski. 1992. *Development of hand skills in the child.* Bethesda, MD: American Occupational Therapy Association, Inc.

Case-Smith, J. 2005. *Occupational therapy for children.* St. Louis: Elsevier Mosby.

Early Childhood Today. 1998. Learning to read and write: Developmentally appropriate practices for young children. *Early Childhood Today.* October, 1998.

Exner, C. E. 2005. Development of Hand Skills. In J. Case-Smith Eds., *Occupational Therapy for children.* p. 304-355. St. Louis, MO: Elsevier.

Gardner, M. F. 1996. *Test of visual motor skills Revised.* Hydesville, CA: Psychological and Educational Publications, Inc.

Henderson, A., & Pehoski, C., Eds. 2006. *Hand function in the child: Foundations for remediation.* St. Louis, MO: Mosby.

Isbell, C., & Isbell, R. 2005. *The inclusive learning center book for preschool children with special needs.* Silver Spring, MD: Gryphon House.

Isbell, R. 2008. *The complete learning centers book Revised.* Silver Spring, MD: Gryphon House.

Klein, M. D. 1990. *Pre-scissor skills.* San Antonio, TX: Therapy Skill Builders.

Klein, M. D. 1996. *Pre-writing skills.* San Antonio, TX: Therapy Skill Builders.

Parham, L. D. & L.S. Fazio. 2007. *Play in occupational therapy for children.* St. Louis: Mosby.

Thelen, E., & Smith, L. 1994. *A dynamic systems approach to the development of cognition and action.* Cambridge, MA: MIT Press.

Trawick-Smith, J. 1997. *Early childhood development: A multicultural perspective.* Upper Saddle River, NJ: Merrill.

Tseng, M. H., & Cermack, S. A. 1993. The influence of ergonomic factors and perceptual-motor abilities on handwriting performance. *American Journal of Occupational Therapy, 4710,* 919-926.

Tseng, M. H., & Chow, S. M. K. 2000. Perceptual-motor function of school-age children with slow handwriting speed. *American Journal of Occupational Therapy. 541,* 83-88.

Weil, M., & Amundson, S. J. 1994. Relationship between visual motor and handwriting skills of children in kindergarten. *American Journal of Occupational Therapy. 48,* 982-988.

Index

A

American Sign Language, 34

B

Bilateral coordination, 50, 60, 72, 99,
Bilateral hand skills, 8, 13, 21, 29, 31–34, 58–59, 89,
  92, 99, 119, 122, 131–132
    defined, 135

C

Charting skills, 21
Child Find Program, 134
    defined, 135
Clipboards, 35
Cognitive development, 8, 131
    defined, 135
Counting activities, 41-42, 58, 92, 104, 108, 110
Cultural considerations, 11
Cutting materials, 26, 131

D

Descriptive language, 73, 80, 86, 93, 117–118
Developmental readiness, 12
Developmentally appropriate practices, 9, 15, 29
    defined, 135
Digital pronate grasp, 30
    defined, 135
Directional terms, 74, 88
Drawing skills
    five-year-olds, 98, 118
    four-year-olds, 62, 80, 83, 85, 87
    three-year-olds, 34–35, 51
Drawing tools, 9, 30, 35, 61, 80, 83, 118
    choosing, 25–26
Dressing skills, 7, 20, 132
    five-year-olds, 123
    four-year-olds, 65
Dynamic tripod grasp, 30, 62, 98, 132
    defined, 135

E

Environment, 17–27
    learning centers, 20–23
    literacy-rich, 19
    materials, 19–20, 25–27
    Plexiglas art wall, 23
Experimentation, 9
Eye-hand coordination, 8, 13, 21, 26, 132
    defined, 135
    five-year-olds, 98, 100–104, 109–110, 112, 119,
      121, 123–124, 127
    four-year-olds, 64–67, 76, 81, 88–89, 93
    three-year-olds, 31, 36–37, 41, 43, 47–49, 56,
      58–59

F

Fine motor center, 21–23, 117
    props for, 24
Fine motor skills
    defined, 135
    for preschoolers, 8
    pre-writing skills, 14–15
    pre-scissor skills, 15–16
    teachers' role, 17
    importance of, 7–8
    developing, 9–13
    developmental sequence, 10–11
    foundations of, 11–13
Finger coordination
    four-year-olds, 66
    three-year-olds, 42, 49
Finger isolation
    defined, 135
    five-year-olds, 104
    four-year-olds, 66, 75
    three-year-olds, 34, 52
Finger strength
    five-year-olds, 99, 105, 108, 114
    four-year-olds, 75
    three-year-olds, 36, 39
Five-year-olds, 97–129
    milestones, 98
Forearm/wrist control, 13
    three-year-olds, 40, 51
Four-year-olds, 61–95
    milestones, 62

G

Gender, 11
Grasp, 8, 13, 23, 25, 131–132
    defined, 135
    five-year-olds, 98, 105–108, 115, 126, 128–129
    four-year-olds, 68–73, 75
    three-year-olds, 29, 37–41, 51
Gross motor skills, 11–12
    defined, 135
    three-year-olds, 50

H

Hand dominance/handedness, 131
    defined, 135
Hand strength
    five-year-olds, 115
    four-year-olds, 68, 73–75, 81
    three-year-olds, 26, 33, 38, 42–43, 46, 48–49
Home living center, 20, 105, 116, 123, 127

I

Incline boards, 70, 82
Individuals with Disabilities Education Act, 135
In-hand manipulation, 8
    defined, 135
    five-year-olds, 98–99, 109–111

J

Journaling, 19, 83

L

Labeling, 19, 98, 110
Large motor skills. *See* Gross motor skills
Learning centers, 20–23
Letter formation, 19, 23, 132–133
    five-year-olds, 97–98, 100–102, 105, 111–115
    four-year-olds, 81, 83, 85, 87, 95

M

Multi-sensory activities, 114
Muscle tone, 11

O

Occupational therapists
    defined, 135
Open-ended activities
    defined, 135
Outdoor activities, 35, 48, 54, 87, 93, 107

P

Pencil grasp, 12, 18, 25, 131–132
    correcting, 133
    defined, 135
    five-year-olds, 97, 100, 105–108, 113, 116, 126,
      128–129
    four-year-olds, 82–83
Pencil grips, 133
    defined, 135
Pencils, 19, 24–25, 62, 83, 116, 119, 121, 127, 129
    choosing, 131
    golf, 24–25, 107, 115–116, 131
Pincer grasp
    defined, 136
    five-year-olds, 110
    four-year-olds, 70–72
    three-year-olds, 37–39, 41, 57
Posture, 12, 22
    three-year-olds, 40
Pre-scissor skills, 11, 21
    developing, 15–16
    four-year-olds, 69, 76–79, 94–95
    three-year-olds, 30, 44–49
Pre-writing skills, 11, 13, 21, 132
    developing, 14–15
    developmental steps, 18–19
    five-year-olds, 98, 102, 105, 111–116
    four-year-olds, 80–88
    guiding, 18
    three-year-olds, 50–55
Proprioceptive sense, 8
    defined, 136

Q

Quadripod grasp, 98, 132
    defined, 136

R

Reciprocal hand skills, 10, 13
    defined, 136
Release, 8
    defined, 136
    four-year-olds, 68, 70
    three-year-olds, 41

S

Sand/water table, 20, 37–38, 74
Scaffolding, 17, 98
Scissor skills
    five-year-olds, 98, 103, 118–122
Self-care skills, 7, 20, 30, 65, 97, 123, 132
Self-confidence, 43, 56, 59, 65, 90–91, 114, 127
Shoulder strength, 12, 85
Singing activities, 34, 60, 85, 104, 107
Small motor skills. *See* Fine motor skills
Sorting activities, 33, 40–41, 92, 109–110
Static tripod grasp, 62
    defined, 136
Storytelling, 40, 66, 70, 72, 83, 107, 118, 120
Stringing/lacing skills, 12, 24
    choosing materials, 26–27
    five-year-olds, 123
    four-year-olds, 62, 89–91
    three-year-olds, 30, 44, 56–59
Styluses, 105, 124
    defined, 136
Symbolic representation, 19–20, 62, 98, 116

T

Tactile sense, 8, 55, 115
    defined, 136
Temperament, 11
Three-year-olds, 29–60
    milestones, 30
Tracing skills, 18, 24
    five-year-olds, 109
    four-year-olds, 70, 79, 81, 84, 86–87
    three-year-olds, 55
Trust, 17

U

Upper body strength, 12, 85
    four-year-olds, 85
    three-year-olds, 29, 35, 60

V

Vertical surfaces, 23, 40, 46, 51, 54, 84, 106
Visual skills, 8

W

Writing backwards, 132
Writing tools, 13, 19, 24, 61, 79–80, 82, 97, 113, 115,
   127
    choosing, 25–26